Excel
Breakthrough

Dramatically increase your speed, productivity and efficiency

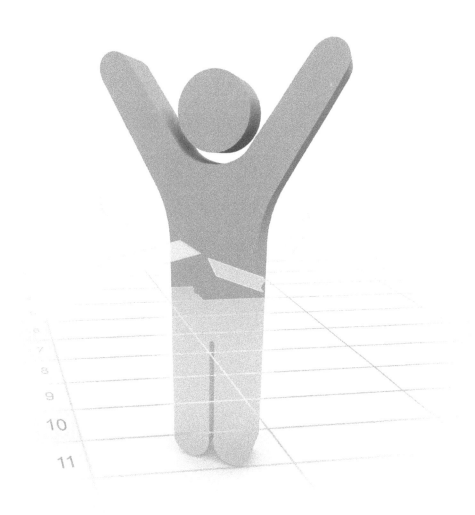

Excel Breakthrough

Dramatically increase your speed, productivity and efficiency with Microsoft Excel.

By Jeremy Miller

JMG, Inc.   Sherman Oaks, CA

This book is dedicated to everyone who is ready to have a breakthrough using Microsoft Excel efficiently and being able to quickly solve complex, tedious tasks with ease, often without using the mouse!

Published by
JMG, Inc.
14622 Ventura Blvd. Suite 102-715
Sherman Oaks, CA 91403

To order
JMG, Inc.
14622 Ventura Blvd. Suite 102-715
Sherman Oaks, CA 91403
http://www.excelbreakthrough.com
orders@excelbreakthrough.com

Logo and cover art design: Trudeau Creative

Editorial and production services: Editide

ISBN: 978-0-9821809-0-7

Table of Contents

Introduction

Do you want to get really good at Excel? Do you want to save time, frustration and become truly *efficient* with Excel? Do you want people to say "Whoa, that's awesome!" when they see how fast you solve complex Excel tasks? Do you want to get done in minutes what takes hours for many Excel users?

If you answered *yes* to any of these questions, then this book is for you.

This book will guide you to having a breakthrough using Excel efficiently and be able to quickly solve complex, tedious data processing tasks with ease, often without using the mouse.

There are many resources for Excel on the Internet, many of which you can buy in the form of books, courses and consulting. There are also many free resources. Indeed, many of the basic commands, tips, tricks and keyboard shortcuts you will find here you can also find scattered around the Internet—if you looked hard enough.

This book will save you time and frustration. It will illuminate your awareness of how these tricks are actually used and how to bring them together in one easy to follow guide full of screenshots from Excel and step-by-step instructions. Think of this more as a power-course than as a book!

What Can You Expect from This Book?

This book is not a comprehensive guide to all possible Excel functionality. Nor is this book merely a list of keyboard shortcuts to make you more efficient. While you will get many tips, tricks and shortcuts in this book that *will* make you a more powerful and efficient Excel user, this book will teach you how to *think clearly* about Excel.

This book will illuminate you to what is known as creative data processing. You will learn to handle complex and tedious data processing tasks in less time than you would ever think is possible. You won't need to download any special Excel add-ins or toolbars or learn Visual Basic programming.

This level of Excel use is similar to what programmers call *elegance*. Elegant computer code does exactly what is needed—no more, no less. It is easy to update. It is properly commented so another programmer can understand it. And ideally it minimizes the amount of processing power the computer must exert. Your use of Excel should be no different. Elegant solutions will get the job done, are easy to understand relative to the complexity of the problem, and they don't leave you completely drained the way tedious manual processing does.

Who Should Read This Book?

This book is intended for anyone who uses Excel who needs to be faster at organizing data, solving problems and working more efficiently with financial and other models. People in the following fields and beyond will absolutely benefit from reading this book:

- Marketing
- Business Development
- Finance
- Sales
- Accounting

- Human Resources
- Research & Development
- IT / MIS
- Academia
- Manufacturing

Additionally, this book is ideal for anyone studying in the following fields:

- Science and Engineering
- Business and Marketing
- Psychology

- Mathematics and Statistics
- Economics

Excel Versions

As of the publication of this book, the latest version of Excel is 12.0, more commonly known as Excel 2007. The most obvious change with Excel 2007 is the interface with its reorganized toolbars and menus at the top. Another major change is that the grid size is much larger. Instead of having 65536 rows by 256 columns like recent Excel versions such as 2003, XP or 2000, Excel 2007 boasts more than 16,000 columns and 1 million rows available.

This book is based on Excel 2000/XP/2003. The reason is because nearly all my clients, both corporate and individual, have not migrated to Excel 2007 and few have plans to do so until some time in late 2008 or 2009.

Just about all of the methods, tips and tricks in this book stay the same for Excel 2007, particularly the ones involving getting around spreadsheets and doing operations without a mouse. More importantly, the core functionality of sorting, filtering, pivot tabling, formulas and the like have not changed dramatically and those methods are at the core of the data processing breakthroughs you will read about here.

Because of the interface and menu changes, some keyboard shortcutting is different, but you can easily learn the new methods by comparing what this book says to what you see in Excel 2007 and substitute where appropriate.

How This Book Is Organized

This book is divided into three parts.

Part 1 – Fundamentals

Part 1 covers key fundamentals about the Excel grid, cells, ranges and a few other features.

Part 2 – Core Lessons

Part 2 goes through each of the core lessons that are critical to having an *Excel Breakthrough*. Remember, these lessons will not be a comprehensive list of all possible Excel possible functionality related to processing data. Instead it is intended to give you a basic understanding of the essential functionality of Excel that, when used in various combinations, will yield your breakthroughs. Complex examples will include step-by-step guides. It is organized by Methods, Functionality and Formulas.

- Methods
  - Control Method—Keyboard shortcuts starting with the Control key
  - Alt Method—Keyboard shortcuts starting with the Alt key
  - Menu Method—Keyboard shortcuts starting with the Menu key (which is essentially the same as clicking the right mouse button)

- Functionality
  - Sorting
  - Filtering
  - Grouping
  - Subtotaling

- Formulas
  - Simple Formulas
  - Nested Formulas

Special note: Many sections of this book will refer to sample Excel files. These files are available at www.excelbreakthrough.com.

Part 3 – Real World Problems

Part 3 is where we use Parts 1 and 2 in solving real problems. Every problem in Part 3 is from a real example from my consulting experience helping Excel users. The data have been purposely changed for non-disclosure reasons, but otherwise these are from actual client challenges. Part 3 is where your transformation from an ordinary Excel user to an *Excel Breakthrough* user will fully emerge.

It is important to remember that Part 3 purposely does not cover every possible data processing scenario. That would be like teaching architecture by having students study blueprints of every building ever constructed. It would be unnecessary and tedious. Instead, Part 3 will spark your mind into understanding that complex data processing can be accomplished with great elegance rather than brute force of lengthy manual effort.

The goal of this book is for you to walk away armed and ready to handle anything thrown at you in Excel with ease. Whether you have to process 5,000 data records in five minutes or reorganize and format data tables in such a way that you are left energized rather than drained, this book will give you powerful tools to handle it all.

Notation Used in This Book

In this book you will see instructions on which keystrokes or key combinations to use to perform a function or execute a command. But before we review that, let's review the basic US QWERTY keyboard layout shown below:

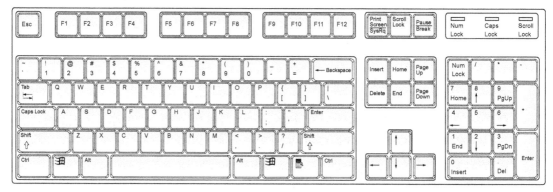

You should already be familiar with this if you use a computer, particularly one running Microsoft Windows. The most important keys for having *Excel Breakthroughs* are the following:

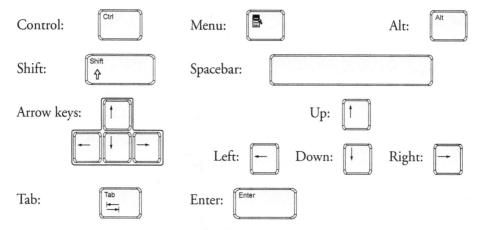

Below are examples of how to read the keystroke instructions you will find in this book. For most Windows and Excel users, these should be familiar:

Instruction you will see in this book:	What it means to do:
Ctrl+C	Hold down Control key and hit C
Alt–E–S–V–Enter	Hit Alt key, then hit E key, then hit S key, then hit V key, then hit Enter key
Menu–D	Hit Menu key, then hit D key
Shift+Space	Hold down Shift key and hit Spacebar
Ctrl+Up	Hold down Control key and hit Up Arrow
Ctrl+Down	Hold down Control key and hit Down Arrow
Ctrl+Left	Hold down Control key and hit Left Arrow
Ctrl+Right	Hold down Control key and hit Down Arrow

Notice in particular that "Ctrl" will be used for "Control key" because the actual key on most US keyboards says "Ctrl."

The most important thing to remember is the difference between + and – in my notation. The + means "hold down first key, then hit second key." The – means "hit the first key and release; hit the second key and release; etc."

Part 1
Fundamentals

If you're eager to see screenshots with detailed instruction lists on how to do all those things I promise this book will offer, don't worry because they are right around the corner in Part 2. Before we get to that we need to cover a few basics about Excel that will be essential for everything you are going to learn here. Be sure not to skip over this, because it will spark your understanding of Excel at the deepest level.

Why is Excel so Special?

Excel is by far the most important and flexible software ever created for the business world. It brings organization in the form of financial models, electronic lists, small databases and so much more. It wasn't the world's first spreadsheet, but for years it has been the standard computer tool for hundreds of millions of people around the world.

Consider the two sets of squares below.

Set 1:

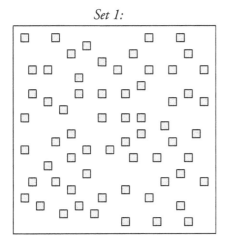

Set 2:

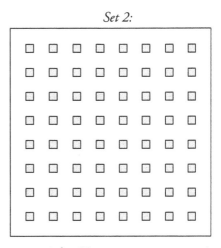

How many squares are in Set 1? It takes some time to count, right? How many squares are in Set 2? It's easier this time, right? It's easy to determine that all the squares are aligned in Set 2, so we just count the number of rows and columns and multiply.

In the same way it is easier to count the squares in Set 2, Excel makes it easy to work with data because of its grid structure. Oh, there are 64 squares in each set.

The Excel Grid

The Excel Grid is visually easy to follow, naturally guiding your eye down and across to bring order to data. It helps us minimize the amount of mental energy required to comprehend data and lock our eyes onto what we need to see. Imagine if the words on this page had no sequence. It would be impossible to read, even though all the words would still be visible.

The ordered row/column structure of the Excel grid is the key to organizing and processing your data. You will always be able to move around in regular rows and columns like a rook on a chessboard using simple keyboard shortcuts. That alone is often enough to transform an otherwise tedious or impossible task into a simple thirty second exercise.

The Excel grid:

	A	B	C	D	E	F	G
1							
2							
3							
4							
5							
6							
7							
8							
9							
10							
11							
12							
13							
14							
15							

Breakthroughs

The key to having a breakthrough in your ability to use Excel (i.e., having an *Excel Breakthrough*) is to understand how to efficiently use your energy to accomplish what you need. Think of your energy as power stored in a battery that is used for all mental and physical tasks related to processing and analyzing data. Thus, when you work with Excel you expend energy by reading data in cells, moving the mouse, hitting keys on the keyboard, moving your hand back and forth from the mouse and keyboard and most critically, figuring out how to handle the data you've been given.

The challenge for many Excel users is that they are simply not aware of numerous hidden ways to be faster and more efficient. Once they do come in contact with certain tips, tricks and shortcuts their use of Excel changes forever. Such will be with you after reading this book. You *will* have an *Excel Breakthrough*.

Muscle Memory

We're almost ready to move into the core lessons that will serve as the foundation for the rest of this book. Before we do, keep in mind that learning *Excel Breakthrough* methods involves simple muscle memory. Many of the basic lessons of Part 2 involve keyboard shortcutting, such as hitting Ctrl+C to copy and then Alt–E–S–V–Enter to paste values. To the unfamiliar these keyboard shortcuts may feel awkward at first but with practice we can execute them with very little thought, just like the way an athlete learns skills via muscle memory.

Anyone who has played a computer or video game implicitly understands that it takes a little time to learn the controls. Excel is no different except that is significantly easier to commit the shortcuts to muscle memory. The problem is that there are keyboard shortcuts that we don't know *we don't even know about!*

Core Concepts

Now we will cover some basic Excel terms, concepts and features that, while you may already be aware of, are critical to know for what's to come in Parts 2 and 3. The core concepts include the following:

- Cells and Ranges
- Active Cell
- Cell and Range Notation
- The Status Bar
- Keyboard Shortcut Fundamentals

Cells and Ranges

The Excel grid is made of *cells* aligned in rows and columns. Have you ever highlighted more than one cell at a time in Excel? That's a range as shown to the right.

A *range* can actually just be one cell, or all the way up to the entire page. Just click and drag. When you have a range highlighted, any actions you take, such as copy, paste, bold, etc., will be implemented over the selected range.

Active Cell

Suppose we have the range of cells highlighted as shown in the previous image under Cells and Ranges. Notice that A1 is white. This is the *active cell* of that range selected. If you hit the Enter key you'll notice the *active cell* moves to the next cell in the range:

At this point if we type something it will show up in A2:

	A	B	C	D
1				
2	Hello			
3				
4				

Cell and Range Notation

While most Excel users already know the following notation, it is important to review it just in case you are *really* new to Excel. Individual cells are referred to by their rows and column headers. A1 refers to the cell in the intersection of row 1 and column A. B1 refers to the intersection of row 1 and column B.

Ranges of cells are referred this way: A1:B3.

	A	B	C	D
1				
2	Hello			
3				
4				

The range B2:G8 is show below.

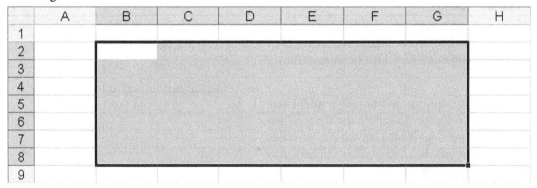

The Status Bar

Excel has a "Status Bar" that runs along the bottom of the Excel window. By default you should always have it visible. Here's what Excel looks like with it visible:

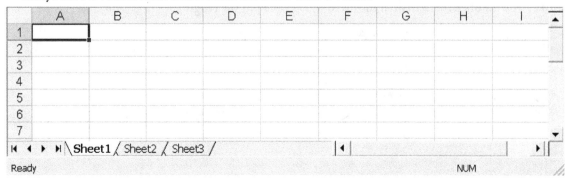

And here is what it looks like with the Status Bar invisible:

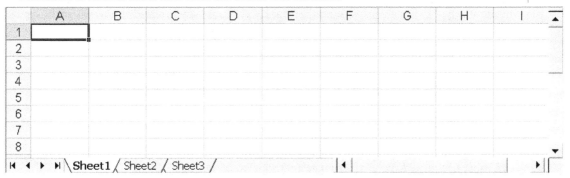

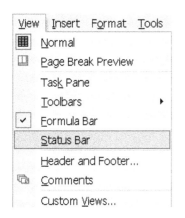

If the Status Bar is not visible, go to the View menu and select Status Bar, as shown at left.

Also, you can go to Tools…Options and click on the View tab. Make sure the "Status bar" box is checked and hit OK.

The Status Bar provides information in the lower left of the screen about running macros or calculations, as well as a very handy feature when working with ranges. When you highlight a range, the Status Bar can display basic mathematical operations on the cell values in the range and display the result in the Status Bar itself. So for those of you who are new to Excel this functionality does not change anything in your worksheets, as one of my clients was afraid of!

Right click anywhere in the Status bar to bring up this popup menu:

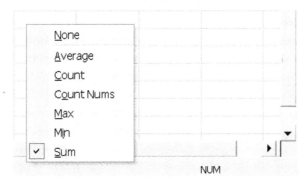

The functions in the screenshot above are the functions available. Then, when you highlight more than one cell with numerical values in it, the right end of the Status Bar will display the result of operating that function over the range you selected.

Usually the most useful function is Sum. But it is also useful to see the Maximum value (Max), the Minimum value (Min), the Count of items (Count) in the range, etc.

This functionality will be used in both Parts 2 and 3.

Keyboard Shortcut Fundamentals

Knowing how to type definitely helps you be faster at Excel because if you already know where the keys are and have that down as second nature, you are going to be able to learn keyboard shortcuts faster.

Whether you know how to type or not, the fact that you are using Excel implies that you at least have some familiarity with the keyboard. When my clients first start learning *Excel Breakthrough* performance, they learn to base their finger movements from the home keys.

The various lessons discussed in Part 2 of this book, particularly the "Methods" such as Control, Alt and Menu, are all dependent on being comfortable with the keyboard. Generally speaking, the areas of the keyboard most useful to *Excel Breakthrough* methods are along the bottom.

What can you do with the keyboard? Most of us already know cut, copy and paste as Ctrl+X, Ctrl+C and Ctrl+V. We see these shortcuts in the menus, and since they are used in all MS Office applications and beyond most people who use a computer are familiar with them.

Other very common keyboard shortcuts most of us know:

Ctrl+O	Open	Ctrl+B	Bold
Ctrl+S	Save	Ctrl+I	Italics
Ctrl+N	New	Ctrl+U	Underline
Ctrl+W	Close document		

The single most important part of having an *Excel Breakthrough* is working without the mouse. And it is no coincidence that the most common questions I get asked about Excel are how I do so many things so quickly with just the keyboard. When you are busy keying in data or formulas, moving your hand away from the keyboard to use the mouse takes time. There's nothing wrong with that, it's just this often breaks the flow of what you are doing and slows you down.

Keyboard shortcuts speed you up. With them you will move around the data in your worksheet, move between worksheets and highlight ranges all without using the mouse. Experienced Excel users usually know at least a few shortcuts and Excel experts don't even think about them because these shortcuts are burned into their muscle memories.

If you recall from the Introduction we foreshadowed three keyboard shortcutting methods:

- Control Method—Keyboard shortcuts starting with the Control key
- Alt Method—Keyboard shortcuts starting with the Alt key
- Menu Method—Keyboard shortcuts starting with the Menu key (which is essentially the same as using the right mouse button)

In addition to the three Methods above, there is a fourth category of keyboard shortcutting techniques that don't entirely fit into one of the categories above but are still important.

Before moving on we need to cover two very simple lessons about the Enter and Tab keys.

Enter and Shift+Enter

(This lesson uses the sample file Getting Around.xls available at www.excelbreakthrough.com.)

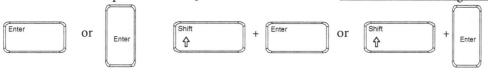

The Enter key is used in Excel in three contexts:

1. Moving up and down and through cells.
2. Cycling through cells in a highlighted range.
3. Equivalent of hitting "OK" in dialog boxes.

Moving Up and Down through Cells

1. When working on a sheet, hitting Enter will take you to the cell beneath the selected cell.
2. Hitting Shift+Enter will take you to the cell above the selected cell.

Cycling through Cells in a Highlighted Range

1. Suppose you have the range A4:E6 selected with A4 as the active cell.

	A	B	C	D	E
1					
2					
3					
4	1	4	7	10	13
5	2	5	8	11	14
6	3	6	9	12	15
7					

2. Hitting Enter will keep the A4:E6 range selected but shift the active cell to A5.

	A	B	C	D	E
1					
2					
3					
4	1	4	7	10	13
5	2	5	8	11	14
6	3	6	9	12	15
7					

3. With A5 as the active cell in this range, hitting Shift+Enter will shift the active cell back up to A4.

It sounds really basic, but many people use the mouse to select each new cell when entering a long list of data. Instead they could simply hit Enter.

Note: If a range is highlighted, such as A4:E6, hitting an Arrow key will select the adjacent cell from the active cell depending on which Arrow key was hit. This happens whether the cells in the range have contents or not.

Tab and Shift+Tab

(This lesson uses the sample file `Getting Around.xls` available at www.excelbreakthrough.com.)

The Tab key is used in Excel in three contexts:

1. Moving left and right through cells.

2. Cycling right or left through the cells in a highlighted range.

3. Cycling through options and components of dialog boxes.

Moving Left and Right through Cells

1. When working on a sheet, hitting Tab will take you to the right the selected cell.

2. Hitting Shift+Tab will take you to the left of the selected cell.

Cycling Right or Left through the Cells in a Highlighted Range

1. Suppose you have the range A4:E6 selected with A4 as the active cell.

	A	B	C	D	E	F
1						
2						
3						
4	1	4	7	10	13	
5	2	5	8	11	14	
6	3	6	9	12	15	
7						

2. Hitting Tab will keep the A4:E6 range selected but shift the active cell to B4.

	A	B	C	D	E	F
1						
2						
3						
4	1	4	7	10	13	
5	2	5	8	11	14	
6	3	6	9	12	15	
7						

3. With B4 as the active cell in this range, hitting Shift+Tab will shift the active cell back to A4.

Cycling through Options and Components of Dialog Boxes

The Tab key is most useful in dialog boxes because it saves the time and mental energy to visually locate and select the option or drop down box, etc. you are looking for. We'll see *many* examples of this later in the book and eventually you will do it without much thought.

Part 2
The Lessons

Now we are going to move more quickly. Part 2 assumes you know the basics introduced in Part 1. If you have used Excel for any reasonable amount of time you will likely know much of what Part 1 presented already. At this point, anything that didn't sink in fully will get reinforced in Part 2.

Here are the lessons:

- Lesson 1 – Keyboard Shortcutting: Control Method
- Lesson 2 – Keyboard Shortcutting: Alt Method
- Lesson 3 – Keyboard Shortcutting: Menu Method
- Lesson 4 – Keyboard Shortcutting: Other Shortcuts
- Lesson 5 – Review of Keyboard Shortcutting Essentials
- Lesson 6 – Excel Functionality
- Lesson 7 – Formulas

Lesson 1 – Keyboard Shortcutting: Control Method

This lesson teaches by far the most powerful keyboard shortcut Method of all: Control Method. You will learn to get around the blocks of data in your worksheets without using the mouse as well as highlight, insert and delete ranges mouse free.

The specific components of Control Method include:
- Getting Around Cells and Ranges
- Selecting Ranges
- Fill
- Highlighting Rows and Columns
- Selecting All Cells on a Worksheet
- Deleting Cells
- Inserting Cells
- Easy Zooming
- Undo/Redo
- Format Painter
- Grouping Worksheets

Getting Around Cells and Ranges

(This lesson uses the sample file `Getting Around.xls` available at www.excelbreakthrough.com.)

One of the most time consuming aspects of working with Excel is getting around the spreadsheet when you need to edit formulas, enter/delete data, add comments, or apply formatting. Using the mouse is obviously a great way to quickly select a specific cell or a range, however there are mouse-free ways that are often much quicker, mainly using Control with Arrow keys which fall under "Control Method."

Control + Arrow Key

Holding Ctrl and pressing an Arrow key will select the next break in empty or non-empty cells.

Ctrl+Up takes you up to the start or end of the next block of non-empty cells.

Ctrl+Down takes you down to the start or end of the next block of non-empty cells.

Ctrl+Left takes you left to the start or end of next the block of non-empty cells.

Ctrl+Right takes you right to the start or end of the next block of non-empty cells.

Consider the following sample spreadsheet from `Getting Around.xls`:

	A	B	C	D	E	F	G	H	I	J
1										
2										
3										
4	1	4	7	10	13		16		19	
5	2	5	8	11	14		17		20	
6	3	6	9	12	15		18		21	

The selected cell is A1. Notice there is no text in rows 1, 2, or 3. Excel is programmed to detect where the next change in empty or non-empty cells is. In this case when starting in A1 and hitting Ctrl+Down, Excel does the following "reasoning" behind the scenes:

Cell A1 is selected. The user hit Ctrl+Down. A1 is empty. A2 is empty. Because A2 has the same "empty/non-empty" status as A1, move onto A3. A3 is empty. Because A3 has the same "empty/non-empty" status as A2, move onto A4. A4 is non-empty. Because A4 is start of non-empty cells, select A4.

	A	B	C	D	E	F	G	H	I	J
1										
2										
3										
4	1	4	7	10	13		16		19	
5	2	5	8	11	14		17		20	
6	3	6	9	12	15		18		21	
7										

In this example, when you start in A1 and you hit Ctrl+Down you select A4 instantly. While using the mouse to select A4 when you already have A1 selected doesn't take much effort, you will start to see how powerful this Control Method is and begin to use it all the time.

Staying in A4, look to the right in row 4. Notice cells A4:E4 are *non-empty*, F4 is *empty*, G4 is *non-empty*, H4 is *empty* and I4 is *non-empty*. If you hit Ctrl+Right when you have A4 selected it will take you to E4. The Excel "reasoning" is as follows:

Cell A4 is selected. The user hit Ctrl+Right. A4 is non-empty. B4 is non-empty. C4 is non-empty. D4 is non-empty. E4 is non-empty. F4 is empty! Thus, E4 is the end of the current block of non-empty cells. Select E4.

	A	B	C	D	E	F	G	H	I	J
1										
2										
3										
4	1	4	7	10	13		16		19	
5	2	5	8	11	14		17		20	
6	3	6	9	12	15		18		21	
7										

With cell E4 selected in our scenario, what would happen if you hit Ctrl+Right again?

Cell E4 is selected. The user hit Ctrl+Right. E4 is non-empty. F4 is empty. G4 is non-empty. Thus, G4 is the start of a block of non-empty cells. Select G4.

	A	B	C	D	E	F	G	H	I	J
1										
2										
3										
4	1	4	7	10	13		16		19	
5	2	5	8	11	14		17		20	
6	3	6	9	12	15		18		21	
7										

With G4 selected in our scenario, if you hit Ctrl+Right again it will take you to I4.

	A	B	C	D	E	F	G	H	I	J
1										
2										
3										
4	1	4	7	10	13		16		19	
5	2	5	8	11	14		17		20	
6	3	6	9	12	15		18		21	

So far we have just moved right using Ctrl+Right but this method works moving up, down and left. The best way to get familiar with it is to practice.

Make sure you are familiar with this technique. Use a worksheet you have saved from work or your personal files. Use the Ctrl+Arrow key combinations to move around the spreadsheet. Play with it. Don't move on until it comes automatically to you. Every scenario covered in Part 3 of this book uses this method.

End Key

The End key, usually positioned above the Arrow keys somewhere, works similarly to Ctrl+Arrow key combinations. When you hit the End button, notice that in the lower right of the screen on the Status Bar the word "END" appears. This means that Excel is in "End Mode" where any Arrow key pressed will select whatever cell a Ctrl+Arrow key combination would have selected.

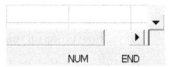

End-Up takes you up to the start or end of the next block of non-empty cells.

End-Down takes you down to the start or end of the next block of non-empty cells.

End-Left takes you left to the start or end of the next block of non-empty cells.

End-Right takes you right to the start or end of the next block of non-empty cells.

Remember, Ctrl+Up means "hold Ctrl and hit Up" and End-Up means "hit End and then hit Up".

While this functionality is useful, the Ctrl+Arrow key method introduced above makes End-Up virtually obsolete.

Control + End

If you hit Ctrl+End you will select the "last cell" in your workbook area. Excel detects two things when you hit Ctrl+End:

1. The last row down the sheet with at least one cell with data or a formula in it.
2. The last column out to the right with at least one cell with data or a formula in it.

With the row and the column detected, Excel selects that cell. If your spreadsheet only had data and formulas in the range A4:I6, Excel would go to I6 when you hit Ctrl+End.

	A	B	C	D	E	F	G	H	I	J
1										
2										
3										
4	1	4	7	10	13		16		19	
5	2	5	8	11	14		17		20	
6	3	6	9	12	15		18		21	
7										

Keep in mind that if your "last cell" was I6, but then you were to delete everything in column I and everything in row 6, hitting Ctrl+End would still take you to I6 because Excel remembers what your "working area" of the worksheet is. If you saved your file, closed it and reopened, Excel would forget that I6 had content in it and instead, when you hit Ctrl+End, would detect what the new last row and last columns are.

Control + Home

It's often very useful to get back to cell A1. When working with long lists or tables of information, you may need to "get back to the top" to reorient yourself to the beginning of the data for some reason. That's where pressing Ctrl+Home is useful. It will select A1 no matter what else you have selected or how far down or right you have scrolled in your workbook. Thus, we can call A1 the "home" cell.

Selecting Ranges

(This lesson uses the sample file Getting Around.xls available at www.excelbreakthrough.com.)

Control + Shift + Arrow Key

Now that you can get around a worksheet without the mouse, the most powerful use of this ability is selecting ranges. The basic rule here is to simply add the Shift key to your Ctrl+Arrow key maneuvers. That's all you do.

Recall the *Getting Around Example* above. Imagine if all our actions were Ctrl+Shift+Arrow key? Instead of just changing the selected cell, you would highlight ranges as you went.

Now consider this next example below, also using Getting Around.xls:

	A	B	C	D	E	F	G	H	I
1									
2									
3									
4	1	4	7	10	13		16		19
5	2	5	8	11	14		17		20
6	3	6	9	12	15		18		21
7									
8	A	B	C	D	E				
9	F	G	H	I	J				
10	K	L	M	N	O				
11	P	Q	R						
12	S	T	U						
13	V	W	X						
14	Y	Z							

Notice we are starting in A1. What if we wanted to highlight only the numbers in the range A4:E6?

1. From A1, hit Ctrl+Down to select A3.

	A	B	C
1			
2			
3			
4	1	4	7
5	2	5	8

2. Hit Ctrl+Shift+Right to select the range A4:E4

	A	B	C	D	E
1					
2					
3					
4	1	4	7	10	13
5	2	5	8	11	14
6	3	6	9	12	15

3. Hit Ctrl+Shift+Down to select A4:E6.

	A	B	C	D	E
1					
2					
3					
4	1	4	7	10	13
5	2	5	8	11	14
6	3	6	9	12	15
7					

Now you have your range A4:E6 highlighted. But what happens if we hit Ctrl+Shift+Right again?

	A	B	C	D	E	F	G	H	I
1									
2									
3									
4	1	4	7	10	13		16		19
5	2	5	8	11	14		17		20
6	3	6	9	12	15		18		21
7									
8	A	B	C	D	E				
9	F	G	H	I	J				
10	K	L	M	N	O				
11	P	Q	R						
12	S	T	U						
13	V	W	X						
14	Y	Z							

Notice the selection extends over A4:G6. From here, if we hit Ctrl+Shift+Down, Excel will recognize the active cell is still A4 and scan down to the next break in column A which is at A8. Thus hitting Ctrl+Shift+Down when in the situation above would yield the following:

	A	B	C	D	E	F	G	H	I
1									
2									
3									
4	1	4	7	10	13		16		19
5	2	5	8	11	14		17		20
6	3	6	9	12	15		18		21
7									
8	A	B	C	D	E				
9	F	G	H	I	J				
10	K	L	M	N	O				
11	P	Q	R						
12	S	T	U						
13	V	W	X						
14	Y	Z							

You may be asking yourself what the point of all this is. Imagine your data range that you needed to highlight was A4:G500. How long would it take you to use the mouse to highlight that range manually? What if your range was A4:G5000? Think how much faster using Control Method is than the mouse.

Control + Shift + End
From wherever your active cell is, hitting Ctrl+Shift+End will highlight from there to the "last cell" in your worksheet. Think of this as doing Ctrl+End but with highlighting.

Control + Shift + Home
Hitting Ctrl+Shift+Home will highlight from the current active cell back up to cell A1.

Fill

(This lesson uses the sample file `Fill.xls` available at www.excelbreakthrough.com.)

This is one of simplest but most power abilities of Excel. Below we see the Fill sub-menu under the Edit menu.

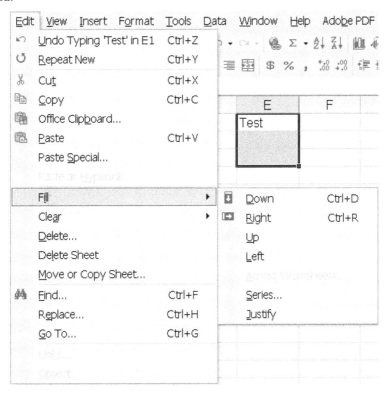

Fill can save you the time it takes to retype the same formula (or text, data, etc.) over and over again. Most experienced Excel users already know this but it's worth mentioning because executing this with keyboard shortcuts is an essential component of the lessons in Part 3 of this book. Because there are many different instances in which you'd want to use this, we'll only cover the basic ones here. Practicing Fill on your own and going through the examples in Part 3 will drive it home for you.

Fill Down

Consider the screenshot at right:

	A	B	C	D
1	**Product**	**Units**	**Revenue**	**Price/Unit**
2	A	23	430	
3	B	76	790	
4	C	43	1029	
5	D	83	1432	
6	E	4	94	
7	F	38	920	
8	G	52	539	
9	H	64	640	

Suppose you need to compute the price per unit for each product (A through H) over the range D2:D9. All you do is type in the right price formula in D2 as shown at right:

SUMIF   ▼ ✗ ✓ f_x =C2/B2

	A	B	C	D
1	**Product**	**Units**	**Revenue**	**Price/Unit**
2	A	23	430	=C2/B2
3	B	76	790	
4	C	43	1029	
5	D	83	1432	
6	E	4	94	
7	F	38	920	
8	G	52	539	

At this point you hit Enter and the formula is set. To get the formula in the rest of the cells in D3:D9 from D2, simply highlight the range D2:D9 as shown …

D2   ▼ f_x =C2/B2

	A	B	C	D
1	**Product**	**Units**	**Revenue**	**Price/Unit**
2	A	23	430	18.6956522
3	B	76	790	
4	C	43	1029	
5	D	83	1432	
6	E	4	94	
7	F	38	920	
8	G	52	539	
9	H	64	640	

… and hit Ctrl+D to *fill* the formulas down to D9:

D2   ▼ f_x =C2/B2

	A	B	C	D
1	**Product**	**Units**	**Revenue**	**Price/Unit**
2	A	23	430	18.6956522
3	B	76	790	10.3947368
4	C	43	1029	23.9302326
5	D	83	1432	17.253012
6	E	4	94	23.5
7	F	38	920	24.2105263
8	G	52	539	10.3653846
9	H	64	640	10

Fill Right

Filling right works basically the same as filling down except it fills formulas out right on the sheet. Consider the following example:

	A	B	C	D	E	F	G	H	I
	K12		▼	fx					
1	Product	A	B	C	D	E	F	G	H
2	Units	23	76	43	83	4	38	52	64
3	Revenue	$430	$790	$1,029	$1,432	$94	$920	$539	$640
4	Price/Unit								

Now suppose you want to fill in the price per unit in for products A through H over the range B4:I4. Type in the price formula for product A in cell B4:

	A	B	C	D	E	F	G	H	I
	SUMIF		▼ X ✓ fx =B3/B2						
1	Product	A	B	C	D	E	F	G	H
2	Units	23	76	43	83	4	38	52	64
3	Revenue	$430	$790	$1,029	$1,432	$94	$920	$539	$640
4	Price/Unit	=B3/B2							

Once the formula is set, highlight the range B4:I4:

	A	B	C	D	E	F	G	H	I
	B4		▼	fx =B3/B2					
1	Product	A	B	C	D	E	F	G	H
2	Units	23	76	43	83	4	38	52	64
3	Revenue	$430	$790	$1,029	$1,432	$94	$920	$539	$640
4	Price/Unit	$19							

Now hit Ctrl+R to fill in the formulas out to I4:

	A	B	C	D	E	F	G	H	I
	B4		▼	fx =B3/B2					
1	Product	A	B	C	D	E	F	G	H
2	Units	23	76	43	83	4	38	52	64
3	Revenue	$430	$790	$1,029	$1,432	$94	$920	$539	$640
4	Price/Unit	$19	$10	$24	$17	$24	$24	$10	$10

Keep in mind that Fill commands are essentially *Copy* commands. You are copying the formula/text/value *and* formatting from the source cell down or across the range. Sometimes you may not want to copy the formats, so be aware that you may need to reset the formatting of the filled range.

Highlighting Rows and Columns
(This lesson uses the sample file Getting Around.xls available at www.excelbreakthrough.com.)

Often we want to do something to an entire row or column at a time.

1. Shift + Space will highlight the entire row(s) of whatever cell (or range) you currently have selected.

2. Control + Space will highlight the entire column(s) of whatever cell (or range) you currently have selected.

At this point you may be asking why we are covering this under Control Method, particularly when the shortcut to highlighting a row does not use the Control key. The reason is that my clients almost always see highlighting rows and columns using only keyboard shortcuts as a logical extension of Control Method.

The most common uses of these two shorcuts are to Insert, Delete, Clear or Format entire rows or columns at a time.

But keep in mind that <u>if you have a range of cells selected, these shortcuts will highlight all columns or rows in your selected range</u>. Examples:

1. Suppose you have **A4:E6** selected:

	A	B	C	D	E
1					
2					
3					
4	1	4	7	10	13
5	2	5	8	11	14
6	3	6	9	12	15

   a. Hit Shift+Space.
   b. Notice this selects all of rows **4:6** as show below:

	A	B	C	D	E	F	G	H	I
1									
2									
3									
4	1	4	7	10	13		16		19
5	2	5	8	11	14		17		20
6	3	6	9	12	15		18		21
7									

2. From here, try hitting Ctrl+Shift+Down. Notice it does the following:

	A	B	C	D	E	F	G	H	I
1									
2									
3									
4	1	4	7	10	13		16		19
5	2	5	8	11	14		17		20
6	3	6	9	12	15		18		21
7									
8	A	B	C	D	E				

3. Hit Ctrl+Shift+Down again:

	A	B	C	D	E	F	G	H	I
1									
2									
3									
4	1	4	7	10	13		16		19
5	2	5	8	11	14		17		20
6	3	6	9	12	15		18		21
7									
8	A	B	C	D	E				
9	F	G	H	I	J				
10	K	L	M	N	O				
11	P	Q	R						
12	S	T	U						
13	V	W	X						
14	Y	Z							

Notice it grabs all the rows to the end of the block of content in row **14**.

4. Reselect only A4:E6.

    a. Hit Ctrl+Space to select all of columns A:E.

	A	B	C	D	E
1					
2					
3					
4	1	4	7	10	13
5	2	5	8	11	14
6	3	6	9	12	15
7					
8	A	B	C	D	E
9	F	G	H	I	J
10	K	L	M	N	O
11	P	Q	R		
12	S	T	U		
13	V	W	X		
14	Y	Z			

The same basic principles of selecting and highlighting without the mouse that apply to rows apply to columns.

5. With columns A:E selected, hitting Shift+Space will highlight all cells in the worksheet. This happens because every row had at least one cell selected, so Excel extended that selection to all cells in all rows.

This might be a good time to go into Excel and play around with this. The more you experiment with highlighting ranges using combinations of Control, Shift and Arrow key the faster you will get with Excel.

Selecting All Cells on a Worksheet with Control + A

Similar to highlighting entire rows or columns at a time, hitting Ctrl+A will highlight all cells on the worksheet. This is useful if you have a lot of content around a worksheet and you want to perform the same action on all of it at once, especially formatting, clearing formatting or copying and deleting all content of a page.

Keep in mind that when you hit Ctrl+A, you will highlight all cells on the worksheet but the active cell will still be whatever cell you had highlighted *before* you hit Ctrl+A.

Quickly Deleting Cells with Control + Minus

(This lesson uses the sample file Getting Around.xls available at www.excelbreakthrough.com.)

If you want to delete cells and not just the contents of the cells, Ctrl+Minus will do that.

This is usually done when you want to move ranges of data or formulas around without actually copying/pasting or dragging and dropping with the mouse.

Keep in mind that when you delete cells it is as if the selected range will get destroyed from the worksheet and the cells adjacent to the range deleted will slide into place to fill up the empty space. When you do that Excel will ask you in which direction you want to fill up those missing cells.

Consider Getting Around.xls again:

	A	B	C	D	E	F	G	H	I
1									
2									
3									
4	1	4	7	10	13		16		19
5	2	5	8	11	14		17		20
6	3	6	9	12	15		18		21
7									
8	A	B	C	D	E				
9	F	G	H	I	J				
10	K	L	M	N	O				
11	P	Q	R						
12	S	T	U						
13	V	W	X						
14	Y	Z							

Select A4:E6 and hit Ctrl+Minus.

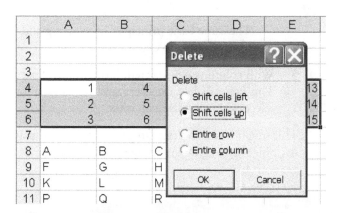

Excel will ask you this no matter how you delete the cells. The main methods are Ctrl+Minus, Edit…Delete from the menus, Menu+D, etc.

If we select "Shift cells up" as shown the result would be:

	A	B	C	D	E	F	G	H	I
1									
2									
3									
4							16		19
5	A	B	C	D	E		17		20
6	F	G	H	I	J		18		21
7	K	L	M	N	O				
8	P	Q	R						
9	S	T	U						
10	V	W	X						
11	Y	Z							

Play around with this. After a few minutes this should become intuitive.

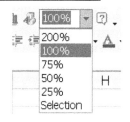

Quickly Inserting Cells with Control + Plus

Ctrl+Plus works in the same way Ctrl+Minus works except it *inserts* cells. And when you do that Excel asks you in which direction you'd like to push out the cells you are inserting on top of. As with Ctrl+Minus, use it carefully because inserting cells can impact formulas and spreadsheet lay-out.

Easy Zooming with Mouse Click–Wheel and Control Key

One of the most important tricks to make Excel more usable is quickly zooming in and out of spreadsheets without going to View…Zoom from the menu or by keying in a magnification level in the Standard Toolbar as shown at right.

To quickly change the magnification hold down Control while scrolling up or down with the mouse wheel. It's that easy. Play with it and see how fast it is. It works in most other Windows applications such as MS Word, Internet Explorer and many non Microsoft applications.

Undo/Redo

Most computer users are familiar with Undo/Redo functionality in most office software suites. Microsoft Office and Excel are no different. If you enter a value or execute a function from a menu or change anything else you realize was a mistake, you can just undo it by hitting Ctrl+Z. This is the same shortcut for Undo as in most Windows document processing applications from Notepad to Powerpoint. And if you decide you that the last action you undid was actually want you wanted to do, just hit Ctrl+Y to Redo.

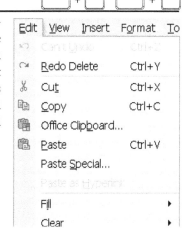

Format Painter

(This lesson uses the sample file `Format Painters.xls` available at www.excelbreakthrough.com.)

Note: Although Format Painter is an Excel feature that is only accessible with the mouse, there are specific keyboard techniques used in conjunction with it, thus we will cover it under Control Method.

Sometimes we don't always want to copy formulas or values and formatting at once. In fact, there are situations where we only want to copy the *formatting* of one range to another. When you have manually set the number format, cell shading, font, font size and border of one range, and *then* you realize you need the exact same formatting on another range that already has values or formulas in it, you might want a faster way to set formats than doing it manually again.

In short, you may want to copy only the formatting of a range to another range without copying the values or formulas.

Excel lets you do this with the Format Painter, a tool only available in the Standard toolbar. The Format Painter button looks like the following:

While the Format Painter does much of what the Paste Special[1] function does (when selecting to only paste formats), the Format Painter is more flexible with the size and range you are pasting the formats into. In other words, the size and shape of the source range does not have to be the same as the destination range. Follow this example below to understand how Format Painter works.

From `Format Painter.xls`, consider the "Format Painter Basic" tab:

	A	B	C	D
1	1		100	
2	2		200	
3	3		300	
4	4		400	
5	5		500	
6	6		100	
7	7		200	
8	8		300	
9	9		400	
10	10		500	
11				

---

[1] We'll get to Paste Special later in Part 2!

1. Highlight the range A1:A10 and apply the Comma Style to it by selecting the Comma button from the Formatting toolbar. It's just to the right of the % button.

2. Then hit Ctrl+B to bold the range. A1:A10 will look like the following:

	A	B	C	D
1	**1.00**		100	
2	**2.00**		200	
3	**3.00**		300	
4	**4.00**		400	
5	**5.00**		500	
6	**6.00**		100	
7	**7.00**		200	
8	**8.00**		300	
9	**9.00**		400	
10	**10.00**		500	
11				

3. With A1:A10 selected, hit the Format Painter Button. Notice your range has the animated dashed outline as if you had copied it. Well, you sort have copied it, except you have only copied the Formatting.
   a. From here, *the next range you select will get the same formatting applied to it!*

4. Since we're still in Format Painter mode, click cell C1.
   a. The range C1:C10 gets formatted exactly as A1:A10 is formatted. Also, Excel automatically highlights the format paste range of the same size and shape as the destination range. Therefore, because your source range is 10 rows by 1 column, Excel highlights 10 rows by 1 column starting with C1.

	A	B	C	D
1	1.00		100.00	
2	2.00		200.00	
3	3.00		300.00	
4	4.00		400.00	
5	5.00		500.00	
6	6.00		100.00	
7	7.00		200.00	
8	8.00		300.00	
9	9.00		400.00	
10	10.00		500.00	
11				

Once you click on the Format Painter button the mouse pointer will put a small paintbrush next to it. When you selected C1 you exited out of Format Paste mode and the mouse pointer returned to normal and the dashed border around A1:A10 disappeared.

Using the Format Painter with Adjacent Ranges

(This lesson uses the "Adjacent Ranges" tab from the file `Format Painter.xls` available at www.excelbreakthrough.com.)

Suppose if in the example above it looked like the image below the data in C1:C10 was actually in B1:B10.

	A	B	C
1	1	100	
2	2	200	
3	3	300	
4	4	400	
5	5	500	
6	6	100	
7	7	200	
8	8	300	
9	9	400	
10	10	500	
11			

If we applied the same formatting to A1:A10, then highlighted the range and then hit the Format Painter (just like last time) you'd see this:

Notice the active cell is A1. If we simply hit the Right Arrow key, Excel will paste the formats to B1:B10 *exactly as if we selected B1 with the mouse.* Format Painter works by pasting the copied format to a range of the same shape starting with where you select. If you select that destination range by using an Arrow key, then it works just as well. It's up to you how you select that destination range.

Using Format Painter with Different Shaped Ranges

(This lesson uses the "Different Shapes" tab from the file `Format Painter.xls` available at www.excelbreakthrough.com.)

Now suppose we wanted to paste the format of A1:A10 into B1:C5. Notice these two ranges are not the same shape:

	A	B	C	D
1	**1.00**	100	100	
2	**2.00**	200	200	
3	**3.00**	300	300	
4	**4.00**	400	400	
5	**5.00**	500	500	
6	**6.00**			
7	**7.00**			
8	**8.00**			
9	**9.00**			
10	**10.00**			

1. Select A1 (and only A1 … we'll see why in a moment) and hit the Format Painter button. We see:

2. With the mouse select B1:C5. Start by clicking on B1 and keep holding down the left
mouse button and drag to C5. With B1:C5 highlighted, let go of the mouse button. This
results in the following:

	A	B	C	D
1	1.00	100.00	100.00	
2	2.00	200.00	200.00	
3	3.00	300.00	300.00	
4	4.00	400.00	400.00	
5	5.00	500.00	500.00	
6	6.00			
7	7.00			
8	8.00			
9	9.00			
10	10.00			

3. Notice the format of A1 painted into the entire range of B1:C5.

Are you starting to see how handy the Format Painter tool is?

Double Clicking the Format Painter Button
(This lesson uses the "Double Click" tab from the file Format Painter.xls available at
www.excelbreakthrough.com.)

By now you might have noticed that when you click the Format Painter button, Excel lets you do
one Format Paste operation. Suppose you wanted to paste the formats of one range into many different ranges of the same size. Consider the screenshot below:

	A	B	C	D	E	F	G
1	1.00		100		100		100
2	2.00		200		200		200
3	3.00		300		300		300
4	4.00		400		400		400
5	5.00		500		500		500

Suppose you wanted to paste the formatting of A1:A5 into C1:C5, E1:E5 and G1:G5. You could do
a normal Format Painter operation 3 times. Or you could:

1. Highlight A1:A5.
2. Double click the Format Painter button. We will be in "Format Painter Mode" where your
mouse cursor has the little paint brush by it until you hit Escape or click on the Format
Painter button again to get out of that mode. However since we are going to stay in Format
Painter Mode …
3. Click on C1. The format of A1:A5 got pasted into C1:C5.
4. Click on E1. The format of A1:A5 got pasted into E1:E5.
5. Click on G1. The format of A1:A5 got pasted into G1:G5.
6. Hit Escape.

Pretty handy, huh?

Grouping Worksheets

(This lesson uses the file Grouping Worksheets.xls available at www.excelbreakthrough.com.)

Suppose we have a workbook with multiple tabs such as the example Grouping Worksheets.xls available at www.excelbreakthrough.com. It has three tabs for three different sales markets:

- SoCal:

	A	B	C	D
1	SoCal			
2	Product	Units	Dollars	ASP
3	Ad-Spy Defense	93,646	$1,557,030	$16.63
4	Audit Deluxe	1,455	$22,075	$15.17
5	Audit Pro	162	$3,275	$20.22
6	Benchmark Tools Pro	53,512	$1,348,141	$25.19
7	Browser Central	14,773	$434,564	$29.42
8	Disk Suite	56,796	$854,382	$15.04
9	Office Tools Basic	98,427	$3,441,471	$34.96
10	Office Tools Elite	2,081,624	$71,105,315	$34.16
11	Photo Organizer	669,661	$20,696,869	$30.91
12	Productivity Bundle	26,301	$652,886	$24.82
13	Security Suite	194,080	$4,271,525	$22.01
14	Spreadsheet Tools	150,936	$3,963,314	$26.26
15	Web Speed Ultra	220,013	$5,628,335	$25.58

- NorCal:

	A	B	C	D
1	NorCal			
2	Product	Units	Dollars	ASP
3	Audit Pro	13,353	$348,419	$26.09
4	Benchmark Tools Basic	51,441	$1,154,754	$22.45
5	Benchmark Tools Pro	263,505	$6,333,539	$24.04
6	Browser Central	151,977	$4,227,865	$27.82
7	Code Cruncher	443,985	$12,819,963	$28.87
8	Disk Suite	2,102	$63,038	$29.99
9	Math Wizard	846,170	$22,323,377	$26.38
10	Office Tools Basic	257,570	$6,353,704	$24.67
11	Office Tools Elite	232,824	$6,239,515	$26.80
12	Office Tools Plus	333,360	$7,817,529	$23.45
13	Office Tools Professional	116,108	$2,943,279	$25.35
14	Photo Organizer	198,625	$3,972,749	$20.00
15	Presentation Spiffer	206,542	$4,176,397	$20.22
16	Productivity Bundle	18,908	$434,911	$23.00
17	Spreadsheet Tools	59,653	$1,620,017	$27.16
18	Spelling Challenge	152,432	$4,146,793	$27.20
19	Virus Begone	185,033	$5,154,569	$27.86
20	Web Speed Ultra	813,164	$26,933,003	$33.12

- PacNW:

	A	B	C	D
1	PacNW			
2	Product	Units	Dollars	ASP
3	Benchmark Tools Basic	15,826	$290,980	$18.39
4	Benchmark Tools Pro	219	$4,269	$19.49
5	Math Wizard	16,187	$293,487	$18.13
6	Office Tools Basic	75,325	$2,220,264	$29.48
7	Office Tools Professional	91,792	$2,339,441	$25.49
8	Productivity Bundle	333	$6,639	$19.94
9	Virus Begone	33,028	$1,120,769	$33.93
10	Web Speed Ultra	7,327	$144,250	$19.69

If we look at the bottom of the workbook we see how the sheets are arranged:

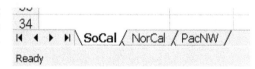

Later we will learn that Ctrl+PgUp and Ctrl+PgDn cycles through active sheets in a workbook. When we add the Shift key into that shortcut, Excel will group tabs together.

1. With the sheet "SoCal" selected as shown above:
   a. Hit Ctrl+Shift+PgDn and notice what happens:
      As shown here, now the "SoCal" and "NorCal" sheets are both selected.

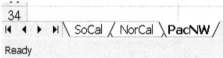

   b. Hit Ctrl+Shift+PgDn again and notice all three are grouped:

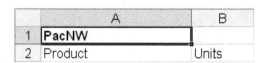

      Now all three sheets are selected.

2. Staying on the "PacNW" sheet ...
   a. Select A1.
   b. Ctrl+B to make A1 bold.

	A	B
1	**PacNW**	
2	Product	Units

3. Now look at the "NorCal" and "SoCal" sheets and notice that cell A1 on both sheets is bold:

	A	B
1	**NorCal**	
2	Product	Units

... and ...

	A	B
1	**SoCal**	
2	Product	Units

When sheets are grouped together, any edit you do to one of the grouped sheets (formatting, formula/data entry or deletion) will occur on all of the grouped sheets.

You can <u>group</u> sheets in three ways:

1. Ctrl+Shift+PgUp or Ctrl+Shift+PgDn.
    a. This method is best for grouping successive sheets in a row when your mind is in "keyboard mode."

2. Hold down Ctrl and click on the exact sheets you want to group.
    a. This method is best for when you want to group some, but not all, of the worksheets and they are not in consecutive order.

3. Right click on any sheet and select "Select All Sheets" as shown:

You can <u>ungroup</u> sheets in 3 different ways:

1. Ctrl+PgUp or Ctrl+PgDn to cycle up or down to a lone sheet.
2. Hold down Ctrl and click on the exact sheets you want to <u>ungroup</u>.
    a. This method is best for when you want to <u>ungroup</u> some, but not all, of the worksheets.

3. Right click on any of the grouped sheets and select "Ungroup Sheets" as shown:

Lesson 2 – Keyboard Shortcutting: Alt Method

The keyboard shortcuts we've gone through fall under what we're calling Control Method, such as Ctrl+X to cut, Ctrl+B to bold or Ctrl+Minus to delete cells. We will also cover the Menu button which we can call the Menu Method of keyboard shortcutting, but before that we must cover Alt Method.

Alt Method means using the Alt button to access the menus without using a mouse.

There are two Alt buttons on standard keyboards on either side of the Spacebar:

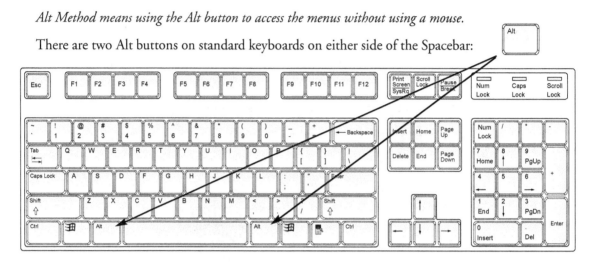

When you hit the Alt button Excel shifts the focus away from the grid and to the menu bar as shown below. Notice how in the menu bar the File menu looks as if your mouse is hovered over it; that's how you know you are actively using the "Alt Method."

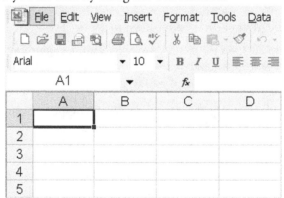

From here, you can *navigate* to any menu item using Arrow keys and *execute* any highlighted menu item with the Enter key. For example, you could copy whatever range you have selected with the following keystrokes:

1. Hit Alt to access the menu bar.
2. Hit Right to move over to the Edit menu.
3. Hit Down four times in a row to select Copy.
4. Hit Enter to execute the Copy command.

Try the above sequence for yourself.

That is a lot of work when you can just use Ctrl+C or Menu–C instead, however there are other very useful functions that have no default Excel keyboard shortcuts that will prove essential in Part 3 of this book.

To get access to the menu sub-items more quickly, you can use the hotkeys for each menu instead of the Arrow keys. Notice that each item in the menu bar has one letter underlined:

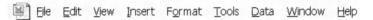

These underlined letters in the menu headers above are "hotkeys." For the File menu, the hotkey is F; for the Edit menu, the hotkey is E; for the Format menu the hotkey is O; etc.

Recall that when you hit the Alt button it will look as if you are holding the mouse over the File menu. (See above). Suppose you hit Alt and then hit E. The Edit menu will appear as as shown at right.

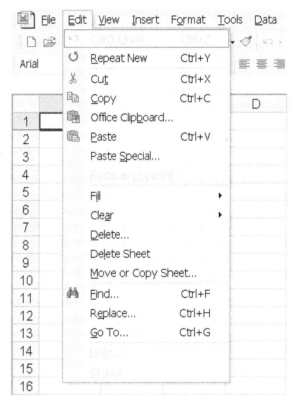

With the Edit menu activated, the active hotkeys become the underlined letters in the menu items pictured, and if you hit the C key you will copy whatever range is selected. If you hit the A key you will access the Clear submenu and hitting D will bring up the Delete dialog box.

Take some time and play with accessing the menu items using Alt Method. While you are not necessarily going to use this method to get to every function, it is very powerful and, as always, it will be used heavily in Part 3 of this book.

The parts we will cover under Alt Method include the following:

- Alt + Down
- Paste Special
- Working with the Menus
- Freeze Panes

Alt + Down

(This lesson uses the file `Staff.xls` available at www.excelbreakthrough.com.)

One time I was moving around a worksheet using the Control Method when I accidentally hit the left Alt key instead of the left Control key. When I hit Alt+Down the active cell I was in spawned a drop down menu from itself with list of data points. I had never seen this before so I was confused. Let me illustrate with the following example.

Suppose we have this simple list of staff members:

	A	B
1	**Staff**	
2	Rob	
3	Mary	
4	James	
5	Richard	
6	Lisa	
7	Peter	
8	Rene	
9	Mike	
10	Terri	
11		

Suppose we select A5 where it says Richard and then we hold down Alt and press Down. We would see the following:

	A	B
1	**Staff**	
2	Rob	
3	Mary	
4	James	
5	Richard	
6	James	
7	Lisa	
	Mary	
8	Mike	
9	Peter	
	Rene	
10	Rob	
11	Terri	

What we see is a simple list box and from here we can use the Arrow keys to highlight any one item up or down the list. When we settle on one we like we can hit Enter and the cell, in this case A5, will change to that value.

When we use Alt+Down, Excel scans the data in the column of the active cell. Excel interprets the column and tries to determine if there is a column header that is distinct from the actual values in the list. In the drop down menu it will display the data values already in the list, and not the header.

The idea is that if you are entering new items into a table you don't have to retype something you've already entered. I personally don't use this that much, however it is somewhat related to Filters which we'll cover later in Part 2.

Paste Special

(This lesson uses the file `Paste Special.xls` available at www.excelbreakthrough.com.)

Alt–E–S is the most powerful Alt Method available. When you do a normal paste operation, Excel pastes everything about the source cell or range you originally copied. This means it pastes the content and the formatting. If the copied range had formulas in it, then the standard paste function will paste the same formulas to the destination range except it will update the ranges, assuming of course the source formulas did not have fixed ranges referenced in them.[2]

Because there is no Excel default shortcut to get to Paste Special, we have to access it from the Edit menu:

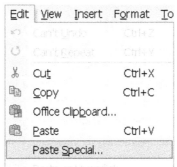

Most Excel users get to this by using the mouse, but with the keyboard all we need to do is hit Alt–E–S which will open up the Paste Special dialog box show below.

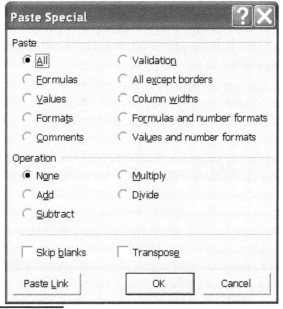

---

[2] We'll see more on fixed ranged references in the Formulas section of Part 2 coming up

Once you are here, notice there are two sections: Paste and Operation. The Paste section is where you tell Excel what you want to Paste. By default it is set to All, meaning paste formulas and formats. The most common use of Paste Special is to paste values without pasting formulas or formats.

To drive home how Paste Special works, read through the following examples and take special note of the keyboard shortcut instructions. All the examples will be based on the following Sales Table:

	A	B	C	D	E	F	G	H
1								
2		Product	Quantity	Price	Pre-Tax	Tax	Total Sale	
3		A	10	$10.00				
4		B	15	$12.00				
5		C	10	$7.50				
6		D	25	$15.00				
7		E	20	$5.00				
8								
9			Tax Rate:	8.25%				

In the table above, there are no formulas yet, just the values you see. I also set range E3:E7 with the same currency format as in the range D3:D7. The purpose of the table is to show the Total Sale value for each product A through E. The formulas in the table are as follows:

Pre-Tax = Quantity * Price

Tax = Quantity * Price * Tax Rate

Total Sale = Pre-Tax + Tax

There are simpler ways of getting Total Sale for each Product without breaking out Pre-Tax and Tax values in their own columns, but for these examples we want to show them.

Example 1: Input Pre-Tax Formulas
(This example uses the "Basic Example" tab from the file Paste Special.xls available at www.excelbreakthrough.com.)

Go to E3 and key in the formula = C3*D3.

E3			fx	=C3*D3				
	A	B	C	D	E	F	G	H
1								
2		Product	Quantity	Price	Pre-Tax	Tax	Total Sale	
3		A	10	$10.00	$100.00			
4		B	15	$12.00				
5		C	10	$7.50				
6		D	25	$15.00				
7		E	20	$5.00				
8								
9			Tax Rate:	8.25%				

For a moment, pretend instead of there being five rows in our table of Products there were actually 5,000. You wouldn't want to manually key in the formula 4,999 more times. Keying it manually four more times isn't so bad, but we're going to use keyboard shortcuts just the same so they get drilled into your brain.

There are several ways we can get the required formulas into E4:E7 without a lot of typing. Starting with E3 as the selected cell (as shown above) and try this:

1. Hit Ctrl+C to copy E3.

2. Highlight the range E3:E7 by:
   a. Hit Left to select D3.
   b. Hit Ctrl+Down to select D7.
   c. Hit Right to select E7.
   d. Hit Ctrl+Shift+Up to highlight E3:E7.

	A	B	C	D	E	F	G	H
1								
2		Product	Quantity	Price	Pre-Tax	Tax		Total Sale
3		A	10	$10.00	$100.00			
4		B	15	$12.00				
5		C	10	$7.50				
6		D	25	$15.00				
7		E	20	$5.00				
8								
9			Tax Rate:	8.25%				

3. Hit Ctrl+V to paste the formulas from E3 through E7.
   a. Notice below that the format of the bottom edge border of E7 changed. This happened because Excel pasted the bottom edge border of E3 along with the formula. That would force us to waste time fixing the formatting.

	A	B	C	D	E	F	G	H
1								
2		Product	Quantity	Price	Pre-Tax	Tax		Total Sale
3		A	10	$10.00	$100.00			
4		B	15	$12.00	$180.00			
5		C	10	$7.50	$75.00			
6		D	25	$15.00	$375.00			
7		E	20	$5.00	$100.00			
8								
9			Tax Rate:	8.25%				

E3				f_x	=C3*D3		

	A	B	C	D	E	F	G	H
1								
2		Product	Quantity	Price	Pre-Tax	Tax	Total Sale	
3		A	10	$10.00	$100.00			
4		B	15	$12.00				
5		C	10	$7.50				
6		D	25	$15.00				
7		E	20	$5.00				
8								
9			Tax Rate:	8.25%				

Starting with E3 selected:

1. Ctrl+C to copy E3.

2. Highlight the range E3:E7:
   a. Left to select D3.
   b. Ctrl+Down to select D7.
   c. Right to select E7.
   d. Ctrl+Shift+Up to highlight E3:E7.

3. Alt–E–S to bring up Paste Special.
   a. Hit the F key to select Formulas as shown:

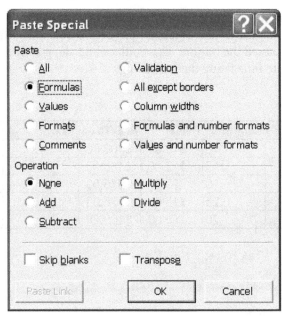

   b. Hit Enter to paste the formulas.

The table will now look like the following:

	E5		▼		ƒx	=C5*D5			
	A	B	C	D	E	F	G	H
1								
2		Product	Quantity	Price	Pre-Tax	Tax		Total Sale
3		A	10	$10.00	$100.00			
4		B	15	$12.00	$180.00			
5		C	10	$7.50	$75.00			
6		D	25	$15.00	$375.00			
7		E	20	$5.00	$100.00			
8								
9			Tax Rate:	8.25%				

The formatting is preserved but the formulas have been correctly pasted.

Example 2: Paste Values

(This example uses the "Basic Example" tab from the file Paste Special.xls available at www.excelbreakthrough.com.)

Suppose for a moment we wanted to do some scratch work with the Pre-Tax values in E3:E7 in another part of the worksheet. Try the following:

1. Copy the range E3:E7.

2. Select E11.

3. Ctrl+V to paste. Here is what we see:

	E11		▼		ƒx	=C11*D11	
	A	B	C	D	E	F
10						
11					$0.00	
12					$0.00	
13					$0.00	
14					$0.00	
15					$0.00	
16						

a. In cell E11 (selected in the image above) we notice that we pasted the formula from E3 and the ranges updated automatically as Excel does by default. Obviously, that wasn't what we wanted, hence in E11:E15 we see all zeros for values.

b. Also note the formatting was pasted. For scratch work that doesn't matter, but for this example let's say we don't want to paste the formatting.

4. Hit Ctrl+Z to undo the paste. E11:E15 will still be selected and E3:E7 will go back to looking like it is copied to the clipboard:

	A	B	C	D	E	F	G	H
1								
2		Product	Quantity	Price	Pre-Tax	Tax	Total Sale	
3		A	10	$10.00	$100.00			
4		B	15	$12.00	$180.00			
5		C	10	$7.50	$75.00			
6		D	25	$15.00	$375.00			
7		E	20	$5.00	$100.00			
8								
9			Tax Rate:	8.25%				
10								
11								
12								
13								
14								
15								
16								

5. Now hit Alt–E–S to bring up Paste Special.

6. Hit V to select Values as shown:

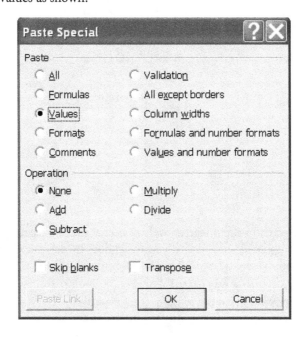

7. Hit Enter to paste *only the values* into E11:E15, and note that only the values, and *not the formulas and formatting*, have been pasted.

E11			▼	*fx* 100		
	A	B	C	D	E	F
10						
11					100	
12					180	
13					75	
14					375	
15					100	
16						

8. Hit Escape to get out of cut/copy/paste mode.

This is the most important use of Paste Special when moving data sets around in complex workbooks where you don't want to paste formulas or formats. I use it all the time. Once you copy the source range, navigate to the destination range and hit Alt–E–S–V–Enter.

When moving data sets between worksheets without pasting the formulas or formats, I select my source range on one sheet, use Ctrl + PgUp or PgDn to get to the sheet I where want to paste. Then I get to cell where I want to paste the range and hit Alt–E–S–V–Enter.

Example 3: Transpose

(This example uses the "Transpose" tab from the file `Paste Special.xls` available at www.excelbreakthrough.com.)

One time I was in a client's office waiting while he had to handle some impromptu work that someone on his staff normally takes care of. He was manually copying and pasting data from columns in one workbook to rows in another workbook. "I hate it when Clint is on the road. It takes me forever to do this," he said. I could see why. He had to do this manual operation on 300 individual cells of data, taking an average of 5 to 10 seconds per cell. That's 1500 to 3000 seconds! What if he had to do 3,000 cells? What about 30,000??

"Have you tried Paste Special—Transpose?" I asked. I explained that Excel can instantly transpose rows or columns of data to the other with Paste Special. We ended up solving his problem in less than 10 seconds instead of taking much longer with his manual way. He was very, very happy.

Suppose we have this table below:

	A	B	C	D
1	Product	Month	Revenue	Units
2	A	Jan	$20	4
3	B	Jan	$54	6
4	C	Jan	$28	7
5	A	Feb	$40	8
6	B	Feb	$90	10
7	C	Feb	$12	3

Now suppose we need it to look like this:

	A	B	C	D	E	F	G	H
8								
9	**Product**	A	B	C	A	B	C	
10	**Month**	Jan	Jan	Jan	Feb	Feb	Feb	
11	**Revenue**	$20	$54	$28	$40	$90	$12	
12	**Units**	4	6	7	8	10	3	
13								
14								

To transpose the table, we do the following:

1. Select A1:D7.
2. Ctrl+C.
3. Select A9. This is just an arbitrary place to paste the transposed table.
4. Alt–E–S to open Paste Special.
5. Hit Tab 3 times. This will move the focus in the Paste Special pop-up to the Transpose checkbox as shown at right:
6. Hit the Spacebar to select Transpose:

7. Hit Enter.

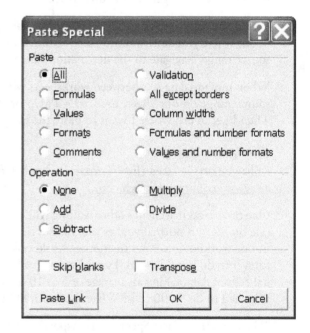

Our worksheet will look like the following:

	A	B	C	D	E	F	G
1	**Product**	**Month**	**Revenue**	**Units**			
2	A	Jan	$20	4			
3	B	Jan	$54	6			
4	C	Jan	$28	7			
5	A	Feb	$40	8			
6	B	Feb	$90	10			
7	C	Feb	$12	3			
8							
9	**Product**	A	B	C	A	B	C
10	**Month**	Jan	Jan	Jan	Feb	Feb	Feb
11	**Revenue**	$20	$54	$28	$40	$90	$12
12	**Units**	4	6	7	8	10	3

Working with the Menus

The File Menu

Using Alt Method with the File menu is a handy method of keyboard shortcutting. The main reason is not only that the F key is close to the Alt key on the keyboard, but it is also close to the C, S and X keys, so a few common shortcut methods can be executed in under a second with the left hand. These shortcuts aren't critical to data processing or analysis, but still they are useful and when you get in the habit of using them you reinforce your facility with using keyboard shortcuts in general.

To see what the shortcuts are, just look at the hotkeys in the File menu at right.

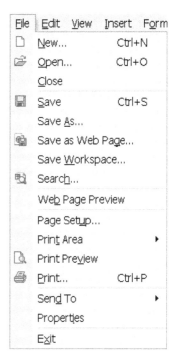

File Menu keyboard shortcut	Action
Alt – F – N (or use Ctrl+N)	Opens a new blank workbook
Alt – F – O (or use Ctrl+O)	Browse for a saved file to open
Alt – F – C (or use Ctrl+W)[3]	Close the active workbook
Alt – F – S (or use Ctrl+S)	Save the active workbook
etc. …	

The most common Alt Method shortcuts I use within the File menu are:

- Alt-F-C to close
- Alt-F-S to save
- Alt-F-X to exit Excel

Some of these shortcuts already have Control Method shortcuts so why would we ever bother to use them? The answer is because the only default way to close Excel without the mouse is Alt–F–X.[4] I often save my file using Alt–F–S, then close my file or Excel using the Alt Method because it is just a little bit faster than switching from Control Method to Alt Method. It sounds trivial, but my clients consistently report that this just makes them feel better about Excel. I find through observation that it helps raise their confidence when they have to do more complex data analysis and manipulation.

Take some time to experiment with using the Alt Method and the File menu.

By now you should be familiar enough with the Alt Method that you can guess that I use it a lot with the other menus as well. We've already introduced the power of Paste Special and how to quickly get to it with Alt–E–S. Now we're going to quickly cover the other menus.

---

[3] Despite the fact that you don't see "Ctrl+W" next to "Close" in the menu, this is the actual Excel keyboard shortcut to close the current workbook that you may already be aware of.

[4] Mac users can use the Command (Apple) button + the Q key, often called "Command+Q" or "Apple+Q" by Mac enthusiasts.

The Edit Menu

Obviously many of the functions available in the Edit menu have
Control Method keyboard shortcuts already, thus learning Alt
Method shortcuts to them may be a little redundant, especially
the basic Cut, Copy and Paste shortcuts. However there are a few
times I use Alt Method with the Edit menu:

- Alt–E–D to delete a range when I'm thinking in "Alt
  Method" (as opposed to using Ctrl+Minus)
- Alt–E–L to Delete Sheet
- Alt–E–M to Move or Copy Sheet …

The View Menu

I typically don't use keyboard shortcuts much with the View menu,
and you can see in the image to the left that there aren't any default
Control Method shortcuts provided by Microsoft. When working
with large data sets, it is often useful to zoom in and out of worksheets which is available from the Zoom option in the View menu,
however I use the Control+Mouse Scrollwheel feature explained
earlier. To refresh your memory, hold down Control and scroll your
mouse's wheel button up and down in Excel and watch the magnification of the sheet zoom in and out.

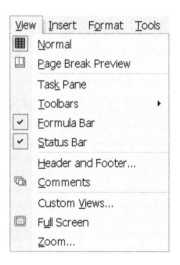

The Insert Menu

As with the View menu, the Insert menu doesn't have many default Control Method keyboard shortcuts, other than to work with Hyperlinks, but that's not very useful when it comes to data processing and analysis. You can insert cells, rows or columns using the mouse right click or by hitting the Menu button and hitting the correct hotkey. The same goes for inserting cell comments. The few Insert menu keyboard shortcuts I like to use are Alt–I–P to insert a picture and Alt–I–M to get to the Name submenu.

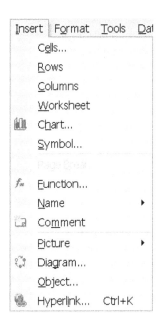

The most useful shortcut is Alt–I–W to insert a new worksheet. Sometimes when you want insert a sheet quickly to do some ad-hoc analysis on data on another sheet it saves mental energy to hit Alt–I–W and copy/paste your data to begin working.

The Format Menu

To get to most items in the Format menu you can just right click the mouse or use the Menu button. Don't worry about the AutoFormat, Conditional Formatting or Style options for now. The most important item in this menu is the first: Cells. But as you can see, you can just use the Ctrl+1 keyboard shortcut to bring up the Format Cells dialog box.

Below are the Format menu and the Format Cells dialog box:

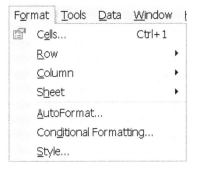
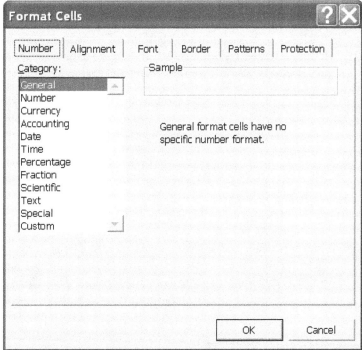

The Tools Menu

The Tools menu has a lot of advanced functionality that, while useful for certain purposes, is not used often enough by most Excel users to warrant a deep discussion here. The most common item on this menu is Options at the bottom. I often use the Alt–T–O shortcut to modify options for various purposes.

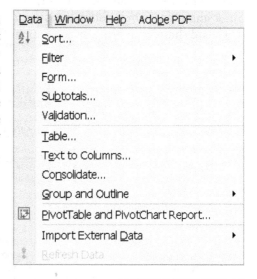

The Data Menu

The Data menu is obviously useful for working with Excel data. I use it all the time and we will go over it in detail in the rest of Part 2 and use it in the examples in Part 3. To access the menu items in the Data menu, you always start with Alt–D. The D key is 2 rows above the left Alt key, so it is very fast to hit the left Alt key with the left thumb and then D with the left middle finger. Try out Alt–D–S and Alt–D–F now and remember you will see these shortcuts again.

The Window Menu

The Window menu is often overlooked, which is unfortunate because it is so useful. As we will see next, using the Alt–W–F to Freeze Panes is very handy when working with large data sets. The Split option is related to Freeze Panes. It does exactly the same thing, except it splits the active worksheet into views that you can scroll through. This allows you to view up to 4 different areas of the same worksheet that are far apart at the same time!

Freeze Panes

(This lesson uses the sample file `Freeze Panes.xls` available at www.excelbreakthrough.com.)

For novices to Excel, this may be a bit confusing at first, but anyone who has used Excel for large tabular reports that extend beyond the visible screen area will appreciate this. In my strategic consulting where I need to present easy to comprehend data sets for my clients, I use this all the time.

Look at this simply formatted data table:

	A	B	C	D	E	F	G	H	I	J
1	Customer	Product	Dec-05	Jan-06	Feb-06	Mar-06	Apr-06	May-06	Jun-06	Jul-
2	Ace Computer	Ad-Spy Defense	21684	2197	1836	2446	5584	682	1272	146
3	Ace Computer	Audit Pro	0	0	0	0	0	0	0	
4	Ace Computer	Audit Standard	0	0	0	0	0	0	0	
5	Ace Computer	Benchmark Tools Basic	0	0	0	0	6396	12572	12553	89
6	Ace Computer	Benchmark Tools Pro	5389	4167	3123	3557	2356	810	1653	12
7	Ace Computer	Browser Central	17623	4100	19828	17734	10353	7991	13239	874
8	Ace Computer	Code Cruncher	0	0	0	0	1640	3973	5934	342
9	Ace Computer	Disk Suite	0	0	0	0	0	0	0	
10	Ace Computer	Math Wizard	9246	2485	1488	1189	1141	834	1514	403
11	Ace Computer	Office Tools Basic	4947	762	652	879	1092	811	2302	248
12	Ace Computer	Office Tools Elite	0	0	39420	14318	5201	3660	7231	548
13	Ace Computer	Office Tools Plus	20443	6406	3149	2282	2180	2140	3833	488
14	Ace Computer	Office Tools Professional	0	0	0	0	0	0	0	
15	Ace Computer	Photo Deluxe	0	0	0	0	0	0	0	
16	Ace Computer	Photo Organizer	0	278	235	521	363	180	320	38
17	Ace Computer	Presentation Spiffer	21700	6024	4105	4228	2336	2334	6927	638
18	Ace Computer	Productivity Bundle	0	0	0	0	0	0	0	
19	Ace Computer	Security Suite	11594	2118	1894	2475	1975	639	1144	259
20	Ace Computer	Speadsheet Tools	0	0	0	0	0	0	0	
21	Ace Computer	Spelling Challenge	0	0	0	0	0	0	0	
22	Ace Computer	Virus Begone	0	0	0	0	0	0	0	
23	Ace Computer	Web Speed Ultra	20220	4538	3826	4517	5088	3217	6104	62

� ◄ ► ▶H \ Month Sales /

Ready   NUM

Notice the data in the table extends below what is visible on the grid. When we use the scroll wheel on the mouse (or use PgDn) to look further down the list, the headers at the top become hidden:

	A	B	C	D	E	F	G	H	I	J
23	Ace Computer	Web Speed Ultra	20220	4538	3826	4517	5988	3217	6104	623
24	Bigtech Commerce	Ad-Spy Defense	0	0	0	0	0	0	0	
25	Bigtech Commerce	Audit Pro	0	0	0	0	0	0	0	
26	Bigtech Commerce	Audit Standard	0	0	0	0	0	0	0	
27	Bigtech Commerce	Benchmark Tools Pro	0	0	0	0	0	0	0	
28	Bigtech Commerce	Browser Central	0	0	0	0	0	0	0	
29	Bigtech Commerce	Code Cruncher	0	0	0	0	0	0	0	
30	Bigtech Commerce	Disk Suite	0	0	0	0	0	0	0	
31	Bigtech Commerce	Office Tools Basic	0	0	0	0	0	0	0	
32	Bigtech Commerce	Office Tools Plus	0	0	0	0	0	0	0	
33	Bigtech Commerce	Productivity Bundle	0	0	0	0	0	0	0	
34	Bigtech Commerce	Security Suite	0	0	0	0	203	193	256	32
35	Computronics	Ad-Spy Defense	68997	21209	24884	29234	26499	15040	28537	2242
36	Computronics	Audit Pro	0	0	0	0	0	0	0	
37	Computronics	Audit Standard	7080	1838	2215	4740	2640	1487	3481	48
38	Computronics	Benchmark Tools Basic	0	0	0	0	0	0	0	
39	Computronics	Benchmark Tools Pro	23148	5607	4498	4282	2782	1930	3049	310
40	Computronics	Browser Central	0	0	0	0	0	0	0	
41	Computronics	Code Cruncher	1196	663	748	658	420	293	632	85
42	Computronics	Disk Suite	17050	5032	3222	2318	1506	817	2255	179
43	Computronics	Math Wizard	0	0	0	0	0	0	0	
44	Computronics	Office Tools Basic	49469	10217	7937	5054	3003	1786	3492	386
45	Computronics	Office Tools Elite	7250	2003	1507	2425	1761	1353	2247	256

� ◄ ► ▶H \ Month Sales /

Ready   NUM

This forces us to remember the headers. That usually means more scrolling back up to remind yourself and then scrolling back down to view your data again. By now you should know I consider this a big waste of mental energy.

Now look at the top of this simply formatted data table again (zoomed in so it shows up more easily):

	A	B	C
1	**Customer**	**Product**	**Dec-05**
2	Ace Computer	Ad-Spy Defense	21684
3	Ace Computer	Audit Pro	0
4	Ace Computer	Audit Standard	0
5	Ace Computer	Benchmark Tools Basic	0
6	Ace Computer	Benchmark Tools Pro	5389
7	Ace Computer	Browser Central	17623

Notice that between rows 1 and 2 the divider line is black instead of gray. That is because we inserted a *Freeze Pane* between rows 1 and 2. Now when we scroll down (shown in the image below) the headers stay frozen. How nice is that?

	A	B	C	D	E
1	**Customer**	**Product**	**Dec-05**	**Jan-06**	**Feb-06**
38	Computronics	Benchmark Tools Basic	0	0	0
39	Computronics	Benchmark Tools Pro	23148	5607	4498
40	Computronics	Browser Central	0	0	0
41	Computronics	Code Cruncher	1196	663	748
42	Computronics	Disk Suite	17050	5032	3222
43	Computronics	Math Wizard	0	0	0
44	Computronics	Office Tools Basic	49469	10217	7937
45	Computronics	Office Tools Elite	7259	2093	1597
46	Computronics	Office Tools Professional	0	0	0
47	Computronics	Photo Organizer	0	0	0

You can insert Freeze Panes from the Window menu using the mouse:

To freeze your column headers:

1. Select the row BELOW the row containing your column labels.
2. Under the Window menu select Freeze Panes.

You can also do this for row labels along the left by freezing columns. To freeze your row labels:

1. Select the column to the RIGHT of the column containing your row labels.
2. Under the Window menu select Freeze Panes.

To freeze both row AND column labels:

1. Select the cell in the row just below your column labels and in the column just to the right of your row labels.
2. Under the Window menu select Freeze Panes.

It is obviously faster to use Alt–W–F than to use the mouse. However, always pay attention to the active cell before using the keyboard shortcut. These examples make it clear:

1. When the active cell is A1, Alt–W–F will do this:

	A	B	C	D	E	F	G	H
1	Customer	Product	Dec-05	Jan-06	Feb-06	Mar-06	Apr-06	May-06
2	Ace Computer	Ad-Spy Defense	21684	2197	1836	2446	5584	682
3	Ace Computer	Audit Pro	0	0	0	0	0	0
4	Ace Computer	Audit Standard	0	0	0	0	0	0
5	Ace Computer	Benchmark Tools Basic	0	0	0	0	6396	12572
6	Ace Computer	Benchmark Tools Pro	5389	4167	3123	3557	2356	810
7	Ace Computer	Browser Central	17623	4100	19828	17734	10353	7991
8	Ace Computer	Code Cruncher	0	0	0	0	1640	3973
9	Ace Computer	Disk Suite	0	0	0	0	0	0
10	Ace Computer	Math Wizard	9246	2485	1488	1189	1141	834
11	Ace Computer	Office Tools Basic	4947	762	652	879	1092	811
12	Ace Computer	Office Tools Elite	0	0	39420	14318	5201	3660
13	Ace Computer	Office Tools Plus	20443	6406	3149	2282	2180	2140
14	Ace Computer	Office Tools Professional	0	0	0	0	0	0
15	Ace Computer	Photo Deluxe	0	0	0	0	0	0
16	Ace Computer	Photo Organizer	0	278	235	521	363	180
17	Ace Computer	Presentation Spiffer	21700	6024	4105	4228	2336	2334
18	Ace Computer	Productivity Bundle	0	0	0	0	0	0
19	Ace Computer	Security Suite	11594	2118	1894	2475	1975	639

Notice above that the panes were frozen between columns F and G and rows 15 and 16. This happened because this was approximately in the middle of the visible rows and columns at the time.

2. When the active cell is A2, Alt–W–F will freeze the row panes between rows 1 and 2 and the column panes will not be frozen at all. We saw this above.
    a. If the active cell is A3, the panes will be frozen between rows 2 and 3.
    b. If the active cell is A4, the panes will be frozen between rows 3 and 4.
    c. Etc.

3. When the active cell is B1, Alt–W–F will freeze the column panes between columns A and B and the row panes will not be frozen at all.

	A	B	C	D
1	Customer	Product	Dec-05	Jan-06
2	Ace Computer	Ad-Spy Defense	21684	2197
3	Ace Computer	Audit Pro	0	0
4	Ace Computer	Audit Standard	0	0
5	Ace Computer	Benchmark Tools Basic	0	0
6	Ace Computer	Benchmark Tools Pro	5389	4167
7	Ace Computer	Browser Central	17623	4100
8	Ace Computer	Code Cruncher	0	0
9	Ace Computer	Disk Suite	0	0
10	Ace Computer	Math Wizard	9246	2485
11	Ace Computer	Office Tools Basic	4947	762
12	Ace Computer	Office Tools Elite	0	0

    a.   Notice the split is between columns A and B.

    b.   If the active cell is C1, the split will between columns B and C.

    c.   See where this is going?

4.   If the active cell is in any column to the left of A *while at the same time* in any row below 1, Alt–W–F will freeze the panes to the left and above that cell.

    a.   So if C6 is the active cell, Alt–W–F will do the following:

	A	B	C	D
1	Customer	Product	Dec-05	Jan-06
2	Ace Computer	Ad-Spy Defense	21684	2197
3	Ace Computer	Audit Pro	0	0
4	Ace Computer	Audit Standard	0	0
5	Ace Computer	Benchmark Tools Basic	0	0
6	Ace Computer	Benchmark Tools Pro	5389	4167
7	Ace Computer	Browser Central	17623	4100
8	Ace Computer	Code Cruncher	0	0

    b.   Notice the split is between rows 5 and 6 and between columns B and C.

Lesson 3 – Keyboard Shortcutting: Menu Method

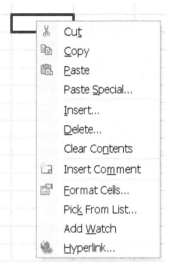

Before we talk about the Menu Method of keyboard shortcutting, we actually need to talk about the mouse! Sometimes when you are using the mouse with one hand and the keyboard with the other you can execute some Excel tasks very efficiently by right clicking the mouse in the Excel grid. This action brings up the context menu shown to the right.

From here, you can use the mouse to select which action to take on the selected range. You can also use a single keystroke to select a function from this menu by pressing the letter on the keyboard that corresponds to the underlined letter in each choice. For example, if you wanted to copy the range you right clicked on, simply hit the C key. To clear the contents of the range, hit the N key. Also, you can simply use the Arrow keys to highlight the option you want and then hit Enter to execute it.

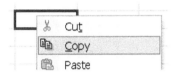

For example, use the Down key to select Copy from the menu and hit Enter to copy the cell as shown to the left.

While using the right click button and selecting an option from the context menu via the mouse or keyboard is certainly efficient, is there a keyboard-only way to do the same thing? Yes! Read on …

The Menu Button

To do the exact same thing as right clicking on a selected range but without using the mouse, simply hit the Menu key, shown here.

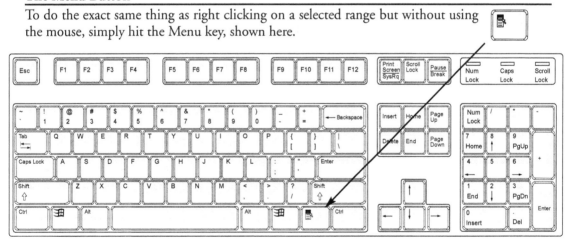

Many of my clients aren't familiar with this key, and often they don't even know where it is on the keyboard. Usually it is located just to the left of the Control key on the right side of the keyboard, i.e., three keys to the right of the Spacebar.

The difference between using the Menu button and right clicking is that you can execute a context menu task without having to take your hands off the keyboard, and that is the most efficient kind of shortcut there is!

Example

Because I am such an Excel junkie, I track all my personal expenses in an Excel workbook rather than in a financial management program. I often enter cell comments on expenses in my checking account tab as I enter transactions. When I do many such entries in a row, to enter a comment I simply hit the Menu key and then hit M to execute the Insert Comment function as shown …

… and here we can see the comment:

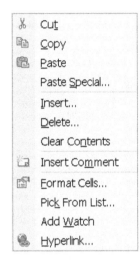

The Menu button is one of the biggest timesavers in many instances, particularly when your right hand is near the Menu button already and you don't want to have to move it to the mouse or a different part of the keyboard and back when you are in a long sequence of data entries or other keyboard shortcuts.

Let's take another look at the context menu that pops up when you right-click or use the Menu button.

Many of our essential editing functions that we execute using the Control or Alt Methods are available here. Of these functions the ones I tend to use most through the Menu Method are:

- Menu–I to Insert the same way as Ctrl+Plus (Control and the "+" key on the right side of the keyboard). I find Menu–I superior because not all laptops have easy to use "+" keys and on full keyboards you still have to move your right hand over to the end of the keyboard. That's just my preference.

- Menu–D to Delete the same way as Ctrl+Minus.

- Menu–M to insert comments. The only other shortcut is to use the Alt Method which I find a little more tedious to remember than Menu–M.

- Menu–F to format cells or a range. The Alt Method alternative is to use Alt–O–E or Alt–O–Enter to get to the Format Cells dialog box. The Control method is to use Ctrl+1. Menu–F is much more logical because the "F" of Format flows much better when you are thinking "I need to *format* this cell."

Lesson 4 – Keyboard Shortcutting: Other Shortcuts

This section covers other keyboard shortcutting methods that don't exactly fit into Control, Alt or Menu Methods. These shortcuts are:

- The Delete key
- Close All Workbooks
- Moving Between Workbooks
- F4 (repeating last action)
- Comparing Data on Two Sheets Very Quickly

The Delete Key

Hitting Delete (also called "Del") will delete the contents of the selected cell or range.

Shift+Delete (or Shift+Del) will cut the cell so it can be pasted elsewhere. In other words, Shift+Del is the same as Ctrl+X.

Close All Workbooks

To close all workbooks open in Excel without quitting the application, hold down the Shift key and open the File menu. Notice that the Close command has been replaced with Close All.

To do this without using the mouse:

1. Hold down Shift.
2. Hit Alt–F–C (while still holding Shift all the way through).

This may be a little awkward at first but it's very handy should the need arise to close many open workbooks at once.

GoTo

Sometimes you may want to get to a specific cell for some reason. You may have a large spreadsheet that you have been using over long enough time such that you can easily recall where some distant piece of data or formula is located in the sheet and you need to get there quickly … *except* you may not want to scroll a bit to get there.

Suppose you knew you needed to get to exactly cell **E500**. Hit Ctrl+G to open the GoTo dialog box shown at right.

Notice in the dialog box that the cursor is in the Reference box. If you start typing, your text will appear there. In this case we enter e500 …

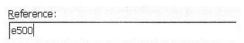

… and hit Enter to take us to cell **E500**.

The great thing about this is that you can use GoTo without ever needing to take your hands of the keyboard.

Moving Between Worksheets

To cycle between worksheets very quickly, use the Control key with either the PageUp or PageDown keys. Take a moment and try this in Excel if you don't know how to do it. My clients who have never known this find it incredibly empowering because they now have a method of going between sheets that doesn't involve the mouse.

The F4 Key (for repeating the last action)

Just a warning: we are going to cover the F4 again later in Part 2 under Formulas regarding setting absolute and relative cell references. For right now, we are going to use the F4 key to repeat the last action you took in Excel.

Consider the following spreadsheet:

	A	B	C
1	1	5	9
2	2	6	10
3	3	7	11
4	4	8	12

Suppose you select B1 and hit Ctrl+Spacebar to highlight all of column B:

	A	B	C	D
1	1	5	9	
2	2	6	10	
3	3	7	11	
4	4	8	12	
5				

Next, suppose you hit Menu–I to insert a blank column:

	A	B	C	D	E
1	1		5	9	
2	2		6	10	
3	3		7	11	
4	4		8	12	
5					

Now if we hit the F4 key Excel will repeat the column insertion because it was the last action taken:

	A	B	C	D	E	F
1	1			5	9	
2	2			6	10	
3	3			7	11	
4	4			8	12	
5						

It is very simple feature most users aren't aware of but it can be very handy when you have to repeat the same task, like inserting or deleting columns several times in a row. If you had to insert 100 blank columns or rows, then it may be a bit tedious but for smaller numbers most of my clients find it very convenient.

Comparing Data on Two Sheets Very Quickly

(This lesson uses the sample file `Comparing Data on Two Sheets.xls` available at www.excelbreakthrough.com.)

Whenever you need to compare data on two different sheets it can sometimes be tedious to go back and forth between sheets comparing data or text. This often comes up when you have lists of data or totals that you want to tie to one another on different pages in a workbook, a common occurrence in financial analysis or quantitative market research.

Suppose we work in a company that breaks down sales territories into "Areas" at the highest level and then breaks these "Areas" into "Regions." Further suppose our company has 4 Areas composed of 5 Regions each, thus 20 Regions in total. Now suppose we have one table of annual sales totals by Area on one sheet and a table of annual sales totals by Region on another.

Areas:

	A	B
1	Area	Units
2	West	9,180,635
3	MidWest	18,503,763
4	South	13,740,770
5	East	2,707,347
6		
7		
8		
9		
10		
11		
12		
13		

\Area / Region /

Regions:

	A	B
1	Region	Units
2	SoCal	3,661,386
3	NorCal	4,346,752
4	PacNW	240,037
5	Mountain South	493,714
6	Mountain North	438,746
7	Chicago Region	1,272,380
8	Minnesota	4,435,210
9	Kansas City	721,056
10	St. Louis	10,059,737
11	Iowa	2,015,380
12	Florida	6,942,412
13	Texas	193,665
14	Gulf	121,322
15	Atlanta	5,712,934
16	Carolinas	770,437
17	NYC	247,898
18	Philadelphia	445,020
19	Washington D.C.	358,616
20	Boston	916,083
21	Pittsburg	739,730

\Area \Region /

If we quickly wanted to tie the total of the Areas to the total of the Regions, here's what we do:

1. Set the Status Bar set to display SUM by right clicking on it and selecting SUM.

None
Average
Count
Count Nums
Max
Min
✓ Sum
NUM

2. On the Areas table, highlight the totals as shown and notice the Sum in the Status Bar is 44,132,515:

	A	B	C	D	E	F	G
1	Area	Units					
2	West	9,180,635					
3	MidWest	18,503,763					
4	South	13,740,770					
5	East	2,707,347					
6							

Area / Region

Ready   Sum=44,132,515   NUM

3. On the Regions table, highlight the totals. Notice Sum=44,132,515 in the Status Bar:

	A	B	C	D	E	F
1	Region	Units				
2	SoCal	3,661,386				
3	NorCal	4,346,752				
4	PacNW	240,037				
5	Mountain South	493,714				
6	Mountain North	438,746				
7	Chicago Region	1,272,380				
8	Minnesota	4,435,210				
9	Kansas City	721,056				
10	St. Louis	10,059,737				
11	Iowa	2,015,380				
12	Florida	6,942,412				
13	Texas	193,665				
14	Gulf	121,322				
15	Atlanta	5,712,934				
16	Carolinas	770,437				
17	NYC	247,898				
18	Philadelphia	445,020				
19	Washington D.C.	358,616				
20	Boston	916,083				
21	Pittsburg	739,730				
22						

Area \ Region

Ready   Sum=44,132,515   NUM

4. Use Ctrl+PgUp or Ctrl+PgDn once. Both are highlighted so you can go back and forth between worksheets very quickly and visually compare the totals.

The advantage of this method ("tying out" in the world of financial reporting and analysis) is that it allows us to keep our eyes focused on one area of the screen while using the keyboard to shift back and forth between pages. If the data does not tie out, the Sums in the Status Bar will be different.

Lesson 5 – Review of Keyboard Shortcut Concepts

We have broken down keyboard shortcutting into three essential Methods: Control, Alt and Menu. Because these Methods all have some overlap, whether you choose to use them along with the mouse is going to depend on how it feels.

For example, you may find that to insert blank columns you like to highlight the column by right clicking the column headers with the mouse to automatically bring up the same context menu that the Menu *button* would, but you then simply hit the I key to insert. The problem with this method is that it requires you to move your hand to the mouse and then move the mouse pointer over the column header.

If you are working in a spreadsheet and don't want to have to do that, you can select a cell in that column using Control Method, then use Crtl+Spacebar to highlight the column and then hit Menu–I to insert a blank column. Personally, I prefer this method as it does not involve the mouse at all.

So the ultimate caveat is that your usage of keyboard shortcuts will vary depending on your preferences. I tell my clients all the time: "If it feels good, do it." Or, "If you can remember it in your muscle memory, go with it."

Three additional points:

- Most people prefer the simple Control Method for doing single key tasks like saving or copy/cut/paste.

- The main distinction between the Control and Alt Methods is that with Control, you have to hold the Control key while pressing another button, which instantly grounds one finger to one button while searching for another button with another finger. Sometimes this causes a little brain drain depending on the general data processing or task you are executing. In that case, Alt Method may actually be less draining because you hit Alt and then forget about it, then hit the next key and forget about it and so forth until you are done.

- Because the Menu button is on the right side of the keyboard, most right handed Excel users tend to use it only when they are not using the mouse while lefties use it more often because their right hand is free from the mouse no matter what.

It sounds insignificant, but based on how you feel about Excel and the keyboard one method or another will be preferable, depending on the situation.

Control Method

The most important Control Method you will want to commit to mental and *muscle* memory first is getting around data in worksheets with the Control and Arrow keys. This alone is a great time and energy saver but is also the foundation for highlighting ranges without the mouse when we add in the Shift key.

Alt Method

The Alt Method allows us to quickly get to all the menu functions not otherwise accessible via Control Method. If you do nothing else with Alt Method, practice using Paste Special. While you can *also* use Menu Method (Menu–S) to get to the exact same Paste Special dialog box, most of my clients seem to prefer using the Alt Method, but both get you to the same place. When you start to use the keyboard to Paste Special more often you will feel so empowered you'll never go back to using the mouse to do it.

Menu Method

The most common use of the Menu button is probably to delete cells with Menu–D, but I have found that my clients tend to find their own favorite uses for the Menu Method depending on what Control or Alt Methods they also prefer.

Lesson 6 – Excel Functionality

With the essentials of keyboard shortcutting under your belt, it's time to move onto the next stage of having an *Excel Breakthrough*: learning Excel's most important data organization functionalities. These include:

- Sorting
  - Via toolbar buttons
  - Via the Data menu
  - Special sort orders
  - Other points about sort options
  - Sorting by more than 3 columns
- Filtering
  - What is a filter?
  - Operating filters without the mouse
  - The "Top 10" filter option
  - Custom filter
  - The Subtotal formula (in conjunction with filters)
- Subtotal in the Data menu
- PivotTables
- Find/Replace
- Text to Columns

Sorting

(This lesson uses the file Sort.xls available at www.excelbreakthrough.com.)

Sorting data is a huge topic, enough to fill up an entire book of its own, but we don't need to exhaust ourselves going through every possible scenario. You know why you want to sort. You want to organize data to find patterns or relationships between records in a table. Sorting is easy, fast and powerful.

The keyboard shortcut to access the sort function isn't necessarily a big time saver, but to sort, I always hit ALT–D–S. It keeps my energy focused on solving the problem, not on thinking about where I have to move the mouse. That may seem trivial, but often I will need to sort data on one sheet to copy and paste it to another sheet. Given the power of keyboard shortcuts to keep you focused and save your mental energy, why interrupt that with the mouse? This is especially true if you are doing many different sort operations on the same data set in a quick sequence. Sometimes you need to look at data sorted several different ways in such a quick sequence to grasp what the data is trying to tell you. It's at this moment that mastering the Sort dialog box without the mouse makes a big difference.

There is another alternative, of course. You can access sort by hitting one of the two Sort buttons from the Standard toolbar:

Sort Ascending: A↓Z   Sort Descending: Z↓A

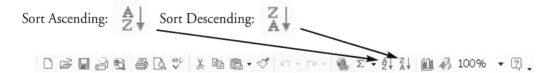

When you sort by using one of these toolbar buttons, Excel automatically scans the worksheet and depending on what it finds and what you have selected it will do different things. Sometimes this is very fast, as Excel won't show you the Sort dialog box—it will interpret what you are doing and just sort. Otherwise you have to select Sort from the Data menu, as shown at right.

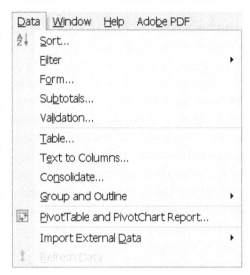

Whether you use the Alt–D–S shortcut or use the mouse to select Sort from the Data menu, Excel will also scan your worksheet and try to determine what you are sorting, automatically highlight the range it thinks you want to sort and then show you the Sort dialog box:

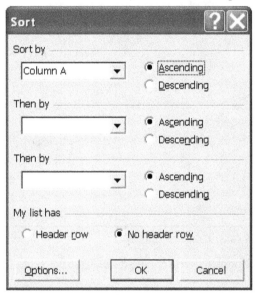

First we'll cover sorting via toolbar buttons and then we'll cover sorting via the Data menu option. For both situations we'll use the following *Product Test Table* that can be found on the "Sort 1" tab of the included file `Sort.xls`:

	A	B	C	D
1	Test Number	Product	Result	
2	1	M	green	
3	2	H	red	
4	3	F	green	
5	4	E	green	
6	5	O	red	
7	6	D	yellow	
8	7	N	green	
9	8	A	yellow	
10	9	L	green	
11	10	P	green	
12	11	B	red	
13	12	G	yellow	
14	13	C	yellow	
15	14	K	green	
16	15	I	red	
17	16	J	green	
18				

Sorting via the Toolbar Buttons

Notice that our Product Test Table above is already sorted by Test Number. Also notice that cells next to the table are all empty. This is important, because when you sort, Excel automatically looks for tables in nicely rectangular shapes. If I had random content in A18:D18 or D1:D18, Excel would interpret that as part of the table and sort it too.

When using the Sort toolbar buttons, make sure the range you want to sort is isolated!

To sort the table alphabetically by Product, select anywhere in the table *in column B* and hit the Sort Ascending button. If we happen to select B4 …

	A	B	C
1	**Test Number**	**Product**	**Result**
2	1	M	green
3	2	H	red
4	3	F	green
5	4	E	green

… and then hit Sort Ascending, the result is:

	A	B	C
1	**Test Number**	**Product**	**Result**
2	8	A	yellow
3	11	B	red
4	13	C	yellow
5	6	D	yellow
6	4	E	green
7	3	F	green
8	12	G	yellow
9	2	H	red
10	15	I	red
11	16	J	green
12	14	K	green
13	9	L	green
14	1	M	green
15	7	N	green
16	5	O	red
17	10	P	green

Here's what Excel did when we hit the Sort button:

1. Scan the range around the selected cell and realize there was a square data table in the range A1:C17.

2. Assume the cells in range A1:C1 were headers in the table and not sort them along with the data in A2:C17. In other words, Excel interpreted A1:C1 as the table's Header Row.

3. Sort the table ascending by Product.

The image at right shows what we would get if we hit Sort Descending instead.

If we had selected a single cell in the range A1:A17 and hit a Sort button, Excel would have sorted our table by Test Number. Select a single cell in C1:C17 and Excel will sort by Result.

Always check the selection before you hit a Sort button!

	A	B	C
1	**Test Number**	**Product**	**Result**
2	10	P	green
3	5	O	red
4	7	N	green
5	1	M	green
6	9	L	green
7	14	K	green
8	16	J	green
9	15	I	red
10	2	H	red
11	12	G	yellow
12	3	F	green
13	4	E	green
14	6	D	yellow
15	13	C	yellow
16	11	B	red
17	8	A	yellow

Suppose in our original table we select B5:C8.

	A	B	C
1	**Test Number**	**Product**	**Result**
2	1	M	green
3	2	H	red
4	3	F	green
5	4	E	green
6	5	O	red
7	6	D	yellow
8	7	N	green
9	8	A	yellow
10	9	L	green
11	10	P	green
12	11	B	red
13	12	G	yellow
14	13	C	yellow
15	14	K	green
16	15	I	red
17	16	J	green

If we hit a sort button Excel will sort *only the range B5:C8* and because B5 is the active cell, Excel will sort by column B. Hitting the Sort Ascending button would result in:

	A	B	C
1	**Test Number**	**Product**	**Result**
2	1	M	green
3	2	H	red
4	3	F	green
5	4	D	yellow
6	5	E	green
7	6	N	green
8	7	O	red
9	8	A	yellow
10	9	L	green
11	10	P	green
12	11	B	red
13	12	G	yellow
14	13	C	yellow
15	14	K	green
16	15	I	red
17	16	J	green

If we hit Sort Descending the result would be:

	A	B	C
1	Test Number	Product	Result
2	1	M	green
3	2	H	red
4	3	F	green
5	4	O	red
6	5	N	green
7	6	E	green
8	7	D	yellow
9	8	A	yellow
10	9	L	green
11	10	P	green
12	11	B	red
13	12	G	yellow
14	13	C	yellow
15	14	K	green
16	15	I	red
17	16	J	green

Sorting via the Data Menu

To perform more powerful Sorts, we have to use the Sort option from the Data menu. As always, I like to access this option with the Alt–D–S shortcut. Once again let's start with our original *Product Test Table*:

	A	B	C	D
1	Test Number	Product	Result	
2	1	M	green	
3	2	H	red	
4	3	F	green	
5	4	E	green	
6	5	O	red	
7	6	D	yellow	
8	7	N	green	
9	8	A	yellow	
10	9	L	green	
11	10	P	green	
12	11	B	red	
13	12	G	yellow	
14	13	C	yellow	
15	14	K	green	
16	15	I	red	
17	16	J	green	
18				

As before, select cell **B4** which is in the Product column and hit Alt–D–S. This brings up the Sort dialog box, but also notice that Excel auto-detected the entire table we are trying to sort:

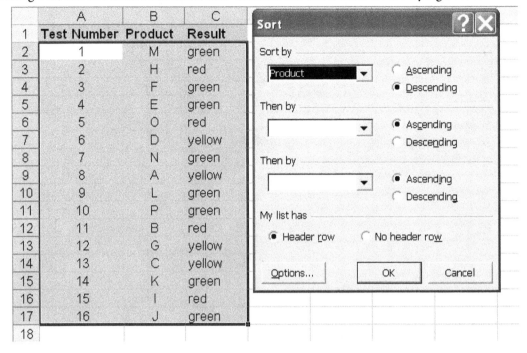

Here's what happened:

1. Excel interpreted the first row of the table as the *Header row*, meaning Excel won't sort the cells in A1:C1 along with the data below. The *Header row* option is automatically checked for us in the Sort dialog box.

2. And because Excel interpreted A1:C1 as the column headers in the table, and because we happened to have sorted the Product column last when we hit Alt–D–S, Excel assumed we still wanted to sort by Product, just as if we had hit one of the Sort toolbar buttons.

Now our attention is on the Sort dialog box and it's very simple to use.

We can sort by multiple columns (up to 3). If you had a table with more than 3 columns and lots of data this is really handy. You simply go from top to bottom and select the column you want to sort by first in the top drop down box, the column you want to sort by after that in the middle drop down box, and the last column you want to sort by after that in the bottom drop down box. With each column, select whether you want to sort Ascending or Descending. Try playing with this with any table of data and you'll find that it's very easy.

Also play with using a header row or not by checking between the two options in the Sort dialog box.

What about using only the keyboard in the Sort dialog box?

As with all Excel dialog boxes, you cycle through and select the drop down boxes and radio buttons in each section using Tab, Arrow keys, Spacebar and hotkeys.

Again suppose we are at this point with our original Product Test Table shown below:

	A	B	C
1	Test Number	Product	Result
2	1	M	green
3	2	H	red
4	3	F	green
5	4	E	green
6	5	O	red
7	6	D	yellow
8	7	N	green
9	8	A	yellow
10	9	L	green
11	10	P	green
12	11	B	red
13	12	G	yellow
14	13	C	yellow
15	14	K	green
16	15	I	red
17	16	J	green
18			

Sort

Sort by

Product ⌄   ○ Ascending   ● Descending

Then by

[ ] ⌄   ● Ascending   ○ Descending

Then by

[ ] ⌄   ● Ascending   ○ Descending

My list has

● Header row   ○ No header row

Options...   OK   Cancel

Notice that the first drop down box is active (where it says "Product"). If we use the Up and Down Arrow keys we can select a different column to sort by as if we were using the mouse, just like you might be familiar with in drop down boxes in other applications or Excel features.

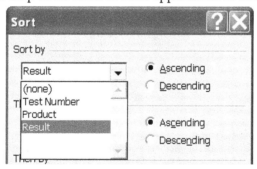

Then we can hit Tab to focus on the Ascending and Descending radio buttons in the first "Sort by" column:

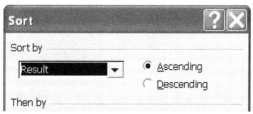

We can select Ascending or Descending with the Arrow keys, or by hitting the hotkeys "A" for Ascending or "D" for Descending. If we hit Shift+Tab we'll cycle back to the first drop down box.

We can navigate the entire Sort dialog box only by using the keyboard if we wanted to. Just try it and you'll see how easy it is. When I sort, I hit Alt–D–S and use my left hand to work the Tab key and my right hand to work the Arrow keys and Shift (in case I need to Shift-Tab backwards to change something I've already been through). At any time if you hit the Enter key it is the equivalent of hitting the OK button in the Sort dialog box. That's how I finish sorting.

Special Sort Orders

Most of the data we sort is composed of numbers or text, and by default Excel sorts numbers 0 to 9 and letters A to Z. If we have letters and numbers mixed in a list, Excel sorts numbers first and then letters. That's all familiar to us, but what if we have a special sequence we want to sort by that doesn't follow these rules? Keep reading …

In our Product Test Table from above, suppose we want to sort by Result. Alphabetically speaking, the order would go green, red and then yellow. But what if we wanted the order to be green, yellow and then red because green meant "good" while yellow meant "moderate" and red meant "bad"? Sorting the table alphabetically would yield the one at right.

	A	B	C
1	Test Number	Product	Result
2	1	M	green
3	3	F	green
4	4	E	green
5	7	N	green
6	9	L	green
7	10	P	green
8	14	K	green
9	16	J	green
10	2	H	red
11	5	O	red
12	11	B	red
13	15	I	red
14	6	D	yellow
15	8	A	yellow
16	12	G	yellow
17	13	C	yellow

If we wanted to see greens first, then yellows, and then reds because we want to go from good to bad, this sort wouldn't work.

The good news is that Excel has a way of mitigating this problem. When you bring up the Sort dialog, click the options box in the lower left corner (or hit Alt–O to use the hotkey) and the Sort Options sub-dialog box will open:

If we select the "First key sort order" drop down menu we see:

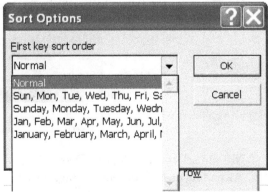

Brilliantly, Excel has a few default lists of common sort sequences that don't follow the Alphabet, namely the days of the week or the months of the year.

Note: this is how you sort by Day or Month in a table with such information. This is very handy!

Obviously we don't see a list with "green, yellow, red" so we'd have to create it somewhere. To do that, we actually have to cancel all the way out of Sort and go to Options under the Tools menu shown at right.

In the Options dialog box select the Custom Lists tab:

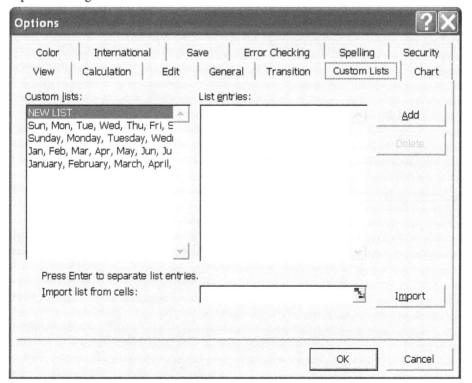

This is where those custom lists came from in the Sort Options picture. Make sure NEW LIST is highlighted as shown above, and in the "List entries" box literally type in "green, yellow, red" as shown at right.

Hit the Add button and your new custom list is now saved.

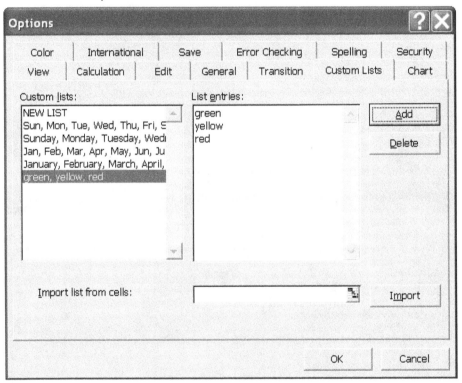

Now go back to our Product Test Table and get to the Sort Options dialog again. This time we see:

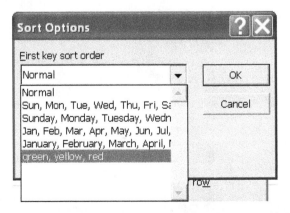

Select that option, hit OK, then you can sort the Result column in our "proper" order rather than alphabetically.

	A	B	C
1	**Test Number**	**Product**	**Result**
2	1	M	green
3	3	F	green
4	4	E	green
5	7	N	green
6	9	L	green
7	10	P	green
8	14	K	green
9	16	J	green
10	6	D	yellow
11	8	A	yellow
12	12	G	yellow
13	13	C	yellow
14	2	H	red
15	5	O	red
16	11	B	red
17	15	I	red

Other Points about Sort Options

1. Sorting by Day:
   a. You can select either "Sun, Mon, Tue, …" or "Sunday, Monday, Tuesday, …."
   b. Make sure that you have the days spelled correctly or else the sort won't work properly.
   c. If you use the abbreviations, make sure you have "Tue" for Tuesday and not "Tues."
   d. Don't have a mix of fully spelled out days and the three letter abbreviations. You have to tell Excel that you want to sort by one way or the other.

2. Sorting by Month:
   a. This follows exactly the same logic as sorting by Day except with Month names and month abbreviations.

Sorting By More than 3 Columns

(This example uses the "Sort 2" tab from the file Sort.xls available at www.excelbreakthrough.com.)

Excel only allows you to sort up to three columns of data at a time. What if we had more than three columns we wanted to sort by? What if our Product Test Table actually had 6 columns instead?

	A	B	C	D	E	F
1	**Test Number**	**Product**	**Result**	**Sessions**	**Tester**	**Location**
2	1	M	green	1	Rob	Lab
3	2	H	red	1	Rob	Lab
4	3	F	green	2	Mary	Floor
5	4	E	green	1	Rob	Floor
6	5	O	red	2	Mary	Lab
7	6	D	yellow	2	Mary	Floor
8	7	N	green	1	Rob	Floor
9	8	A	yellow	2	Mary	Lab
10	9	L	green	2	Rob	Lab
11	10	P	green	1	Mary	Floor
12	11	B	red	1	Mary	Floor
13	12	G	yellow	2	Mary	Lab
14	13	C	yellow	2	Rob	Floor
15	14	K	green	1	Mary	Floor
16	15	I	red	1	Rob	Lab
17	16	J	green	2	Rob	Lab

What if we wanted to sort by Result, Sessions, Tester and Location, in that order? That would mean the highest priority sort order is Result, then Sessions, then Tester, then Location. Also, just assume we want to sort everything in an ascending order.

Here's how to do it:

1. Select any single cell in the Location column of the table (anywhere in F1:F17).
2. Hit Alt–D–S to bring up the Sort dialog box and automatically highlight the table.
3. In the Sort by list select Location, then make sure it's set to Ascending if not already.
4. In first Then by section leave it empty.
5. In the second Then by section leave it empty.
6. Make sure Header Row is selected. It's always good to look at the spreadsheet and make sure the highlighted range is correct.

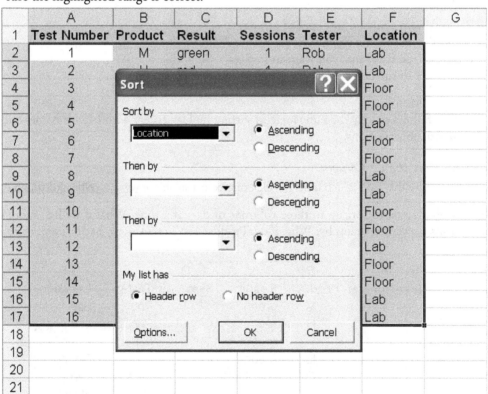

7. Hit OK and now it's sorted by Location.
8. Now hit Alt–D–S again to bring up the Sort dialog box.
9. In the Sort by list select Result.
   a. Select Options and make sure to select the "green, yellow, red" sort order.
10. In the first Then by list select Sessions.
11. In the second Then by list select Tester.
12. Hit Enter.

We have now sorted our table exactly as we want: by Result, then by Sessions, then by Tester, then by Location.

	A	B	C	D	E	F
1	Test Number	Product	Result	Sessions	Tester	Location
2	4	E	green	1	Rob	Floor
3	7	N	green	1	Rob	Floor
4	10	P	green	1	Mary	Floor
5	14	K	green	1	Mary	Floor
6	1	M	green	1	Rob	Lab
7	3	F	green	2	Mary	Floor
8	9	L	green	2	Rob	Lab
9	16	J	green	2	Rob	Lab
10	6	D	yellow	2	Mary	Floor
11	13	C	yellow	2	Rob	Floor
12	8	A	yellow	2	Mary	Lab
13	12	G	yellow	2	Mary	Lab
14	11	B	red	1	Mary	Floor
15	2	H	red	1	Rob	Lab
16	15	I	red	1	Rob	Lab
17	5	O	red	2	Mary	Lab

Filtering

(This lesson uses the file Filter.xls available at www.excelbreakthrough.com.)

Just below Sort on the Data menu is Filter. Filtering is another powerful but easy to use Excel feature.

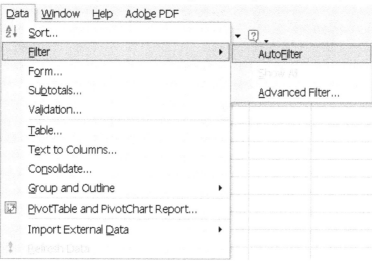

The keyboard shortcut to use a Filter is Alt–D–F–Enter or just Alt–D–F–F. When you hit Alt–D–F you come to the Filter sub-menu in the Data menu as shown above. AutoFilter on the pictured sub-menu is what we're talking about. Don't worry that Excel calls it "AutoFilter" and I'm saying just "Filter" because they mean the same thing.

What is a Filter?

An Excel Filter is a way to focus on subsets of data from a table without actually deleting any cells. It allows you to dynamically hide and unhide rows of data based on desired selection criteria. Common uses of Filtering include:

- You have a big list but only want to focus on certain components.
- You want to enter values in a new column only against certain rows.
- You want to copy a subset of rows from a table to paste somewhere else.
- You want to compute Subtotals[5] based on Filtering.

Recall the Product Test Table from the Sort lesson above:

	A	B	C	D	E	F
1	Test Number	Product	Result	Sessions	Tester	Location
2	1	M	green	1	Rob	Lab
3	2	H	red	1	Rob	Lab
4	3	F	green	2	Mary	Floor
5	4	E	green	1	Rob	Floor
6	5	O	red	2	Mary	Lab
7	6	D	yellow	2	Mary	Floor
8	7	N	green	1	Rob	Floor
9	8	A	yellow	2	Mary	Lab
10	9	L	green	2	Rob	Lab
11	10	P	green	1	Mary	Floor
12	11	B	red	1	Mary	Floor
13	12	G	yellow	2	Mary	Lab
14	13	C	yellow	2	Rob	Floor
15	14	K	green	1	Mary	Floor
16	15	I	red	1	Rob	Lab
17	16	J	green	2	Rob	Lab

What if we only wanted to focus on "green" tests results and not even *look at* any test where the result was red or yellow, but we still didn't want to actually delete the non-green rows? Filters will let you do it. All we need to do is select any single cell in the table and hit Alt–D–F–Enter.[6]

---

[5] We'll talk more about Subtotals soon!

[6] To activate Filters on my data tables in Excel, I always use Alt–D–F–Enter, though keep in mind you can still do Alt–D–F–F. It all depends on what feels right for you. Some of my clients actually report that having to hit F twice a the end of the Alt–D–F–F sequence somehow feels "more draining" than Alt–D–F–Enter, as if hitting Enter makes it more powerful and fun for them. I encourage you to try both and do what ever feels right to you. And maybe using the mouse still feels better to you. Do it your way!

Here's how our table looks after we do that:

	A	B	C	D	E	F
1	Test Numb ▼	Produc ▼	Result ▼	Sessioi ▼	Tester ▼	Locatio ▼
2	1	M	green	1	Rob	Lab
3	2	H	red	1	Rob	Lab
4	3	F	green	2	Mary	Floor
5	4	E	green	1	Rob	Floor
6	5	O	red	2	Mary	Lab
7	6	D	yellow	2	Mary	Floor
8	7	N	green	1	Rob	Floor
9	8	A	yellow	2	Mary	Lab
10	9	L	green	2	Rob	Lab
11	10	P	green	1	Mary	Floor
12	11	B	red	1	Mary	Floor
13	12	G	yellow	2	Mary	Lab
14	13	C	yellow	2	Rob	Floor
15	14	K	green	1	Mary	Floor
16	15	I	red	1	Rob	Lab
17	16	J	green	2	Rob	Lab

Notice in the column headers (A1:F1) at the right end of each cell is a dropdown button (▼). These buttons are how you apply Filters. When you apply a Filter, Excel will only display rows that meet Filter criteria for that column. You can select the Filter buttons directly with the mouse or if you are in the cell with the Filter button, hold down Alt and hit Down. To illustrate, suppose we applied a Filter on the Result column in the above table. So whenever I tell you to select a particular item from a Filter list, you can use either the mouse or the Alt+Down keyboard shortcut.

To apply a Filter to the Results column:

1. Select the Filter button in C1.
   a. As is mentioned in the paragraph above, use the mouse or the Alt+Down shortcut. We'll see the following:

	A	B	C	D	E	F
1	Test Numb ▼	Produc ▼	Result ▼	Sessioi ▼	Tester ▼	Locatio ▼
2	1	M	(All)	1	Rob	Lab
3	2	H	(Top 10...)	1	Rob	Lab
			(Custom...)			
4	3	F	green	2	Mary	Floor
5	4	E	red	1	Rob	Floor
6	5	O	yellow	2	Mary	Lab
			red			
7	6	D	yellow	2	Mary	Floor
8	7	N	green	1	Rob	Floor

Notice the simple drop down menu. Excel automatically populates this with the first three options *All, Top 10 …,* and *Custom ….*

2. Select the option *green* from the drop down menu.

This is what you'll see:

	A	B	C	D	E	F
1	Test Numb ▼	Produc ▼	Result ▼	Sessioı ▼	Tester ▼	Locatio ▼
2	1	M	green	1	Rob	Lab
4	3	F	green	2	Mary	Floor
5	4	E	green	1	Rob	Floor
8	7	N	green	1	Rob	Floor
10	9	L	green	2	Rob	Lab
11	10	P	green	1	Mary	Floor
15	14	K	green	1	Mary	Floor
17	16	J	green	2	Rob	Lab

Notice that the rows with *red* and *yellow* results are hidden; the Filter button in C1 has a blue pointer instead of a black one; and finally, the visible rows in the table have blue numbers in the row labels instead of black numbers. Look closer still and you'll see that where there are hidden rows the line between the row labels is a little thicker.

Compare $\begin{array}{c} 2 \\ \hline 4 \end{array}$ to $\begin{array}{c} 4 \\ \hline 5 \end{array}$. Notice the difference in the gap between **2** and **4** in the first image to the gap between **4** and **5** in the second image. The thicker gap between **2** and **4** in the first image means there is at least one hidden row in between them. We can also deduce that this must be row 3. It's very simple and if you've never tried using a Filter before you'll pick it up very quickly.

From here, we could copy this range and paste it somewhere else. Suppose we selected A1:F17 and copied it:

	A	B	C	D	E	F	G
1	Test Numb ▼	Produc ▼	Result ▼	Sessioı ▼	Tester ▼	Locatio ▼	
2	1	M	green	1	Rob	Lab	
4	3	F	green	2	Mary	Floor	
5	4	E	green	1	Rob	Floor	
8	7	N	green	1	Rob	Floor	
10	9	L	green	2	Rob	Lab	
11	10	P	green	1	Mary	Floor	
15	14	K	green	1	Mary	Floor	
17	16	J	green	2	Rob	Lab	
18							

Notice that the dashed border around the copied cells shows that we didn't copy the cells in the range from the hidden rows. If we select A18 and paste (Ctrl+V) we'll see the following:

	A	B	C	D	E	F	G
1	Test Numb ▼	Produc ▼	Result ▼	Sessiol ▼	Tester ▼	Locatio ▼	
2	1	M	green	1	Rob	Lab	
4	3	F	green	2	Mary	Floor	
5	4	E	green	1	Rob	Floor	
8	7	N	green	1	Rob	Floor	
10	9	L	green	2	Rob	Lab	
11	10	P	green	1	Mary	Floor	
15	14	K	green	1	Mary	Floor	
17	16	J	green	2	Rob	Lab	
18							
19	Test Number	Product	Result	Sessions	Tester	Location	
20	1	M	green	1	Rob	Lab	
21	3	F	green	2	Mary	Floor	
22	4	E	green	1	Rob	Floor	
23	7	N	green	1	Rob	Floor	
24	9	L	green	2	Rob	Lab	
25	10	P	green	1	Mary	Floor	
26	14	K	green	1	Mary	Floor	
27	16	J	green	2	Rob	Lab	

Notice that no rows between 19 and 27 are hidden, meaning that *when* we pasted, we pasted only the visible rows from the original table that we had copied. Consider what a time saver this is.

Now suppose we wanted to focus only on tests with green results that Rob did. We could apply a second filter:

	A	B	C	D	E	F
1	Test Numb ▼	Produc ▼	Result ▼	Sessiol ▼	Tester ▼	Locatio ▼
2	1	M	green	1	(All)	Lab
4	3	F	green	2	(Top 10...) (Custom...)	Floor
5	4	E	green	1	Mary	Floor
8	7	N	green	1	Rob	Floor

And the result would be:

	A	B	C	D	E	F
1	Test Numb ▼	Produc ▼	Result ▼	Sessiol ▼	Tester ▼	Locatio ▼
2	1	M	green	1	Rob	Lab
5	4	E	green	1	Rob	Floor
8	7	N	green	1	Rob	Floor
10	9	L	green	2	Rob	Lab
17	16	J	green	2	Rob	Lab

We could apply as many filters as there are columns of data to isolate exactly what we need.

Operating Filters Without the Mouse

To use a Filter without the mouse, simply select a cell with a Filter button in it (ideally you would select the cell without using a mouse as well) and hit Alt+Down. Then you can use the Up and Down Arrow keys to select the desired Filter option. It's that simple. To be honest, I find that using the mouse is more intuitive and most of my clients prefer that as well.

The "Top 10" Filter Option

I personally don't use Top 10 that much, but it can sometimes be useful when working with columns of numerical data. Top 10 simply shows the top values or percentages from the list. When you select it, it brings up the dialog box shown at right.

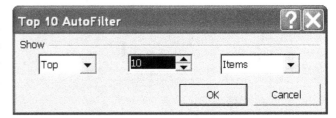

The image above shows that we have three different options to set:

1. Top or Bottom, meaning we can look at the top or the bottom of the list.
2. Then number items from the list or the percent of the Top or Bottom of the list.
3. Items or Percent. If you choose Items then you will select the number of items from the top or bottom of the list that's in the second option.

For example, suppose in our list we only had a filter on Test Number that looked like the one at right.

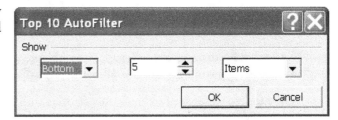

The result would be:

	A	B	C	D	E	F
1	Test Numb ▼	Produc ▼	Result ▼	Sessior ▼	Tester ▼	Locatio ▼
2	1	M	green	1	Rob	Lab
3	2	H	red	1	Rob	Lab
4	3	F	green	2	Mary	Floor
5	4	E	green	1	Rob	Floor
6	5	O	red	2	Mary	Lab

Suppose we wanted the top 25 percent. We would need to set our Filter up like this:

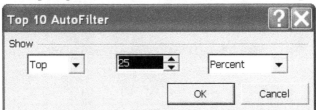

The result would be:

	A	B	C	D	E	F
1	Test Numb ▼	Produc ▼	Result ▼	Sessioı ▼	Tester ▼	Locatio ▼
14	13	C	yellow	2	Rob	Floor
15	14	K	green	1	Mary	Floor
16	15	I	red	1	Rob	Lab
17	16	J	green	2	Rob	Lab

Custom Filter

When we select the *Custom …* option a new dialog box will open. Suppose we selected the Filter button for the Test Number column:

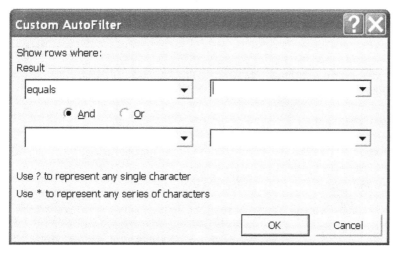

Here we can enter logical arguments to filter for a value or two specific values.

The list on the left has all the arguments (equals, does not equal, is greater than, is less than, contains, does not contain, etc.) and the list on the right allows you to select an item from the pull down menu of the Filter or you can type in a value.

Notice you can select "And" or "Or" between the two rows of requirements. This allows you to determine if the rows you need must meet both ("And") or just one or the other ("Or") of the requirements.

The Subtotal Formula (in conjunction with Filters)

(This lesson uses the file Subtotal Formula.xls available at www.excelbreakthrough.com.)

Although we will cover the bulk of formulas later in Part 2, we're going to cover the Subtotal formula right now because it is a very powerful tool when used with Filters. If you use Excel then you probably know the Sum formula to add values over a range of cells. For example, here is a basic Sum formula in cell A5:

A5	▼		*fx* =SUM(A1:A4)

	A	B	C	D
1	10			
2	5			
3	25			
4	50			
5	90			
6				

The Sum formula is fast and very straight forward. But for other operations the Subtotal function blows Sum out of the water. Subtotal cannot only do addition; it counts, multiplies, averages, finds the maximum or minimum value and even calculates standard deviations or variances from the mean. The syntax is as follows:

    = SUBTOTAL(function_num, ref1, ref2, ref3 . . .)

Function_num is a number 1 to 11 that tells Excel which function you want to use over the references specified in ref1, ref2, ref3, etc.

The functions in the right column of the table to the right are the same as the cell formulas such as SUM or AVERAGE and so forth.

Function_Num	Function
1	AVERAGE
2	COUNT
3	COUNTA
4	MAX
5	MIN
6	PRODUCT
7	STDEV
8	STDEVP
9	SUM
10	VAR
11	VARP

So how is this useful with the Filters? Suppose we have a table of Products, Customers, Units and Dollars as follows:

	A	B	C	D
1	**Product**	**Customer**	**Units**	**Dollars**
2	Ad-Spy Defense	Ace Computer	93,646	$1,557,030
3	Ad-Spy Defense	Bigtech Commerce	398	$8,160
4	Ad-Spy Defense	Computronics	489,698	$11,583,159
5	Ad-Spy Defense	Falcon Retail	104,311	$2,822,940
6	Ad-Spy Defense	Media Edge Interactive	191,106	$4,945,754
7	Ad-Spy Defense	Powertech	35,878	$1,024,073
8	Ad-Spy Defense	R-Tek Tronics	92,862	$2,115,155
9	Ad-Spy Defense	Sygell Distributors	264,091	$7,400,527
10	Ad-Spy Defense	TF General Store	153,322	$4,108,379
11	Audit Deluxe	Media Edge Interactive	1,455	$22,075
12	Audit Deluxe	Powertech	1,344,648	$46,507,451
13	Audit Pro	Ace Computer	248,013	$7,071,200
14	Audit Pro	Bigtech Commerce	162	$3,275
15	Audit Pro	Computronics	16,372	$398,208
16	Audit Pro	Elite Software Sales	13,353	$348,419
17	Audit Pro	Media Edge Interactive	137,797	$3,608,160
18	Audit Pro	R-Tek Tronics	11,328	$160,308
19	Audit Standard	Ace Computer	118,889	$2,146,655
20	Audit Standard	Bigtech Commerce	5,552	$112,885
21	Audit Standard	Computronics	253,538	$7,373,011
22	Audit Standard	Elite Software Sales	201,883	$5,290,071
23	Audit Standard	Falcon Retail	103,671	$2,861,681
24	Audit Standard	Powertech	273,909	$7,679,668
25	Benchmark Tools Basic	Ace Computer	129,537	$3,140,314
26	Benchmark Tools Basic	Computronics	42,065	$1,231,751
27	Benchmark Tools Basic	Elite Software Sales	51,441	$1,154,754

The picture above only shows down to row **27** in Excel but suppose it went all the way down to row **171** as shown:

164	Web Speed Ultra	Elite Software Sales	880,861	$23,729,181
165	Web Speed Ultra	Falcon Retail	130,592	$2,552,176
166	Web Speed Ultra	Media Edge Interactive	112,959	$2,749,240
167	Web Speed Ultra	Powertech	2,167,040	$65,563,214
168	Web Speed Ultra	R-Tek Tronics	113,175	$3,184,926
169	Web Speed Ultra	Station Club	101,452	$2,428,904
170	Web Speed Ultra	Sygell Distributors	249,460	$6,687,291
171	Web Speed Ultra	TF General Store	9,558	$191,248

Suppose we wanted to extract the total Units for a few particular customers. The first thing we do is apply a Filter by hitting Alt–D–F–Enter:

	A	B	C	D
1	**Product** ▼	**Customer** ▼	**Units** ▼	**Dollars** ▼
2	Ad-Spy Defense	Ace Computer	93,646	$1,557,030
3	Ad-Spy Defense	Bigtech Commerce	398	$8,160
4	Ad-Spy Defense	Computronics	489,698	$11,583,159
5	Ad-Spy Defense	Falcon Retail	104,311	$2,822,940
6	Ad-Spy Defense	Media Edge Interactive	191,106	$4,945,754
7	Ad-Spy Defense	Powertech	35,878	$1,024,073
8	Ad-Spy Defense	R-Tek Tronics	92,862	$2,115,155

Then all the way at the bottom in row **173** we put the following formula:

$$=SUBTOTAL(9,C2:C171)$$

C173	▼	f_x	=SUBTOTAL(9,C2:C171)

	A	B	C	D
1	**Product** ▼	**Customer** ▼	**Units** ▼	**Dollars** ▼
169	Web Speed Ultra	Station Club	101,452	$2,428,904
170	Web Speed Ultra	Sygell Distributors	249,460	$6,687,291
171	Web Speed Ultra	TF General Store	9,558	$191,248
172				
173			44,132,515	

Next we go back up to **B1** and use the Filter button to select a customer, say TF General Store:

Customer	▼
(All)	
(Top 10...)	
(Custom...)	
Ace Computer	
Bigtech Commerce	
Computronics	
Elite Software Sales	
Falcon Retail	
Media Edge Interactive	
Powertech	
R-Tek Tronics	
Station Club	
Sygell Distributors	
TF General Store	

The result looks like this:

| C173 | | ▾ | ƒ× | =SUBTOTAL(9,C2:C171) |

	A	B	C
1	Product ▾	Customer ▾	Units ▾
10	Ad-Spy Defense	TF General Store	153,322
30	Benchmark Tools Basic	TF General Store	29,855
54	Code Cruncher	TF General Store	32,429
89	Office Tools Elite	TF General Store	224,436
144	Speadsheet Tools	TF General Store	36,424
171	Web Speed Ultra	TF General Store	9,558
172			
173			486,024

Notice the value displayed in C173 is exactly the sum of the Units *only* for rows with TF General Store as the filtered customer. If we wanted to see the total for another customer, we just select one from the list, such as Falcon Retail:

| C173 | | ▾ | ƒ× | =SUBTOTAL(9,C2:C171) |

	A	B	C	D
1	Product ▾	Customer ▾	Units ▾	Dollars ▾
5	Ad-Spy Defense	Falcon Retail	104,311	$2,822,940
23	Audit Standard	Falcon Retail	103,671	$2,861,681
35	Benchmark Tools Pro	Falcon Retail	498,650	$19,500,317
43	Browser Central	Falcon Retail	14,773	$434,564
51	Code Cruncher	Falcon Retail	321,623	$9,395,010
59	Disk Suite	Falcon Retail	60,808	$906,735
67	Math Wizard	Falcon Retail	671,236	$17,403,895
76	Office Tools Basic	Falcon Retail	206,293	$6,037,537
83	Office Tools Elite	Falcon Retail	135,778	$3,492,376
93	Office Tools Plus	Falcon Retail	10,298	$201,587
98	Office Tools Professional	Falcon Retail	74,280	$2,288,590
110	Photo Organizer	Falcon Retail	175,037	$4,821,452
124	Productivity Bundle	Falcon Retail	22,355	$438,779
132	Security Suite	Falcon Retail	64,188	$1,213,475
139	Speadsheet Tools	Falcon Retail	278,296	$7,576,888
156	Virus Begone	Falcon Retail	184,517	$5,144,377
165	Web Speed Ultra	Falcon Retail	130,592	$2,552,176
172				
173			3,056,706	

What's great about using the Subtotal formula is that we don't have to sort the list and manually grab the sum of the Units each time. We just change the filter, grab the sum and we're done!

Subtotal[7] in the Data Menu

(This lesson uses the file `Subtotal Feature.xls` available at www.excelbreakthrough.com.)

In addition to the Subtotal *formula* covered above, Excel also has a Subtotal *feature* found under the Data menu that is powerful yet often underused.

Suppose we are the sales manager of a software distributor and we have an Excel sheet of product sales results showing Units, Revenues and Average Sales Price (ASP). The sales are broken out by Market (i.e. geographic sales area), Customer and Product. Below only the header row and the first 14 data rows are visible. Assume this table goes all the way down to row 300 and covers all Markets, Customers and Products in our sales system.

	A	B	C	D	
1	**Market**	**Customer**	**Product**	**Units**	
2	Atlanta	Ace Computer	Audit Pro	248,013	
3	Atlanta	Ace Computer	Benchmark Tools Pro	315,256	
4	Atlanta	Ace Computer	Web Speed Ultra	240,230	
5	Atlanta	Bigtech Commerce	Code Cruncher	6,943	
6	Atlanta	Media Edge Interactive	Photo Organizer	52,241	
7	Atlanta	Powertech	Code Cruncher	1,454,652	
8	Atlanta	Powertech	Photo Organizer	1,258,396	
9	Atlanta	Powertech	Presentation Spiffer	968,596	
10	Atlanta	Powertech	Web Speed Ultra	1,100,611	
11	Atlanta	Sygell Distributors	Web Speed Ultra	67,996	
12	Boston	Ace Computer	Presentation Spiffer	52,393	
13	Boston	Ace Computer	Security Suite	20,690	
14	Boston	Computronics	Office Tools Basic	14,517	
15	Boston	Falcon Retail	Disk Suite	4,012	

Notice our table is sorted by Market, then by Customer and finally by Product. Suppose our task is to find the total Units and Sales in each market and display it in some easy to use way. "Easy to use" is open to interpretation, but what the Subtotal feature does is generally considered user friendly by most Excel users.

---

[7] Remember, don't confuse the Subtotal feature from the Data menu with the Subtotal formula covered earlier.

Let's begin by highlighting the entire table[8] and then select to Data ... Subtotals ...

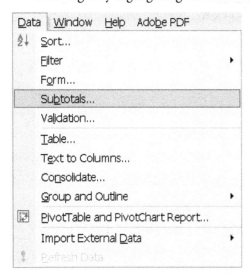

... and we'll see the following dialog box:

For now, we'll leave the "At each change in:" drop-down option set to "Market" and the "Use function:" drop-down set to Sum. In the "Add subtotal to:" box we'll select both Units and Dollars. We'll leave the other options selected as shown above. When we hit OK we see the following:

1 2 3		A	B	C	D	E	F
	1	**Market**	**Customer**	**Product**	**Units**	**Dollars**	**ASP**
	2	Atlanta	Ace Computer	Audit Pro	248,013	$7,071,200	$29
	3	Atlanta	Ace Computer	Benchmark Tools Pro	315,256	$9,093,287	$29
	4	Atlanta	Ace Computer	Web Speed Ultra	240,230	$6,908,122	$29
	5	Atlanta	Bigtech Commerce	Code Cruncher	6,943	$207,283	$30
	6	Atlanta	Media Edge Interactive	Photo Organizer	52,241	$1,550,585	$30
	7	Atlanta	Powertech	Code Cruncher	1,454,652	$43,703,703	$30
	8	Atlanta	Powertech	Photo Organizer	1,258,396	$38,173,678	$30
	9	Atlanta	Powertech	Presentation Spiffer	968,596	$29,140,201	$30
	10	Atlanta	Powertech	Web Speed Ultra	1,100,611	$33,463,333	$30
	11	Atlanta	Sygell Distributors	Web Speed Ultra	67,996	$1,965,646	$29
−	12	**Atlanta Total**			5,712,934	$171,277,038	
	13	Boston	Ace Computer	Presentation Spiffer	52,393	$1,231,459	$24
	14	Boston	Ace Computer	Security Suite	20,690	$548,753	$27
	15	Boston	Computronics	Office Tools Basic	14,517	$366,398	$25
	16	Boston	Falcon Retail	Disk Suite	4,012	$52,353	$13
	17	Boston	Falcon Retail	Office Tools Basic	96,902	$2,883,210	$30
	18	Boston	Media Edge Interactive	Math Wizard	3,540	$106,080	$30
	19	Boston	Media Edge Interactive	Office Tools Professional	20,633	$617,522	$30
	20	Boston	Powertech	Code Cruncher	431,352	$14,911,646	$35
	21	Boston	Powertech	Security Suite	134,519	$4,128,690	$31
	22	Boston	Powertech	Virus Begone	108,614	$3,440,224	$32
	23	Boston	R-Tek Tronics	Office Tools Plus	12,856	$200,930	$16
	24	Boston	R-Tek Tronics	Photo Organizer	16,055	$414,407	$26
−	25	**Boston Total**			916,083	$28,901,672	

---

[8] Subtotal will auto select a table of data in the exact same way the Sort function will, so you don't necessarily need to manually-highlight your dataset first.

Right away we see something is afoot in Excel. The Subtotal function inserted a summary row for each market with the sum of Units and Dollars. For example, in row **12** we see the Atlanta Total. But that's not all. We can also see an outline structure to the left of the row labels. That's where the little buttons with the bold minus sign is. Above all that are little buttons labeled 1, 2 and 3.

1 2 3		A	B	C	D	E	F
	1	**Market**	**Customer**	**Product**	**Units**	**Dollars**	**ASP**
	12	**Atlanta Total**			5,712,934	$171,277,038	
	13	Boston	Ace Computer	Presentation Spiffer	52,393	$1,231,459	$24
	14	Boston	Ace Computer	Security Suite	20,690	$548,753	$27
	15	Boston	Computronics	Office Tools Basic	14,517	$366,398	$25
	16	Boston	Falcon Retail	Disk Suite	4,012	$52,353	$13
	17	Boston	Falcon Retail	Office Tools Basic	96,902	$2,883,210	$30
	18	Boston	Media Edge Interactive	Math Wizard	3,540	$106,080	$30
	19	Boston	Media Edge Interactive	Office Tools Professional	20,633	$617,522	$30
	20	Boston	Powertech	Code Cruncher	431,352	$14,911,646	$35
	21	Boston	Powertech	Security Suite	134,519	$4,128,690	$31
	22	Boston	Powertech	Virus Begone	108,614	$3,440,224	$32
	23	Boston	R-Tek Tronics	Office Tools Plus	12,856	$200,930	$16
	24	Boston	R-Tek Tronics	Photo Organizer	16,055	$414,407	$26
	25	**Boston Total**			916,083	$28,901,672	
	26	Carolinas	Ace Computer	Code Cruncher	30,766	$920,919	$30

If we press the button just to the left of the Atlanta Total in row **12** this happens:

1 2 3		A	B	C	D	E	F
	1	**Market**	**Customer**	**Product**	**Units**	**Dollars**	**ASP**
	12	**Atlanta Total**			5,712,934	$171,277,038	
	13	Boston	Ace Computer	Presentation Spiffer	52,393	$1,231,459	$24

Just like that the Atlanta detail rows are hidden and the button to the left of row **12** has a plus instead of a minus.

Click on a plus to expand, click on a minus to contract.

The 1, 2 and 3 buttons in the top left corner of the image above control the level of detail visible. Also in the image above, we can see that all levels of detail in the table are visible. If we hit the 1 button in the upper left …

… Excel will contract the entire table and hide the second and third levels. Try setting up your own Subtotal table and play around with hitting the buttons. It's easy.

Finally, to remove Subtotals, select somewhere in the table with the Subtotals, go to the Subtotals feature under the Data menu and hit the "Remove All" button.

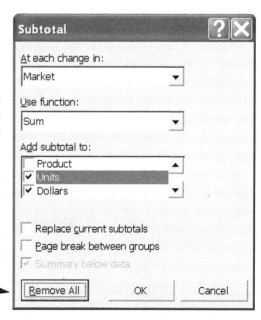

PivotTables

(This lesson uses the file `PivotTable.xls` available at www.excelbreakthrough.com.)

PivotTables were one of the last pieces of Excel functionality that I learned to use well. Because I had worked so much with Excel based interfaces for dimensional databases already, I never had much use for PivotTables in my work until I was forced to use them in grad school. In truth, PivotTables scared me because I knew of other Excel power users who used them all the time and the thought of working with them made me feel a little inadequate. But one day I decided to "bite the bullet" and just get over it. And you know what? It wasn't that bad. If you have "issues" with PivotTables you can get over them, too.

PivotTables handle data in dimensions (rows, columns and headers) that require more complex visual and conceptual reasoning. They sum and organize data into reports independent of the layout of the original table. Right now I'll just show you the basics. We'll see them again in Part 3.

Suppose we have a data table in the range A1:D24 as shown below:

	A	B	C	D
1	Market	Customer	Units	Dollars
2	Mountain North	Ace Computer	110,179	$3,209,606
3	Mountain North	Computronics	93,878	$2,152,708
4	SoCal	Bigtech Commerce	26,463	$656,161
5	Mountain South	Bigtech Commerce	51,585	$1,333,535
6	PacNW	Computronics	219	$4,269
7	NorCal	Falcon Retail	1,257,708	$34,362,575
8	PacNW	Falcon Retail	75,658	$2,226,903
9	SoCal	Computronics	423,602	$11,907,492
10	SoCal	Media Edge Interactive	1,455	$22,075
11	NorCal	Elite Software Sales	718,964	$17,441,987
12	NorCal	Media Edge Interactive	183,191	$5,085,029
13	NorCal	Ace Computer	445,650	$12,884,898
14	Mountain North	Powertech	71,665	$2,370,469
15	NorCal	Bigtech Commerce	29,735	$754,531
16	SoCal	Powertech	2,751,285	$91,802,184
17	PacNW	Media Edge Interactive	51,927	$1,415,957
18	Mountain South	Elite Software Sales	245,813	$6,435,590
19	NorCal	Computronics	151,249	$3,489,469
20	NorCal	Powertech	453,918	$15,716,318
21	Mountain South	Falcon Retail	104,311	$2,822,940
22	SoCal	Falcon Retail	76,194	$1,361,030
23	SoCal	Ace Computer	226,487	$4,147,135
24	PacNW	Ace Computer	21,313	$382,389

Select a cell anywhere in the table and select "PivotTable and PivotChart Report ..." from the data menu. (Alt–D–P)

Because we are selecting a cell in the table to begin with, Excel will guess what you want to run a PivotTable on just like it would for Sorting:

	A	B	C	D
1	Market	Customer	Units	Dollars
2	Mountain North	Ace Computer	110,179	$3,209,606
3	Mountain North	Computronics	93,878	$2,152,708
4	SoCal	Bigtech Commerce	26,463	$656,161
5	Mountain South	Bigtech Commerce	51,585	$1,333,535
6	PacNW	Computronics	219	$4,269
7	NorCal	Falcon Retail	1,257,708	$34,362,575
8	PacNW	Falcon Retail	75,658	$2,226,903
9	SoCal	Computronics	423,602	$11,907,492

PivotTable and PivotChart Wizard - Step 2 of 3

Where is the data that you want to use?

Range: $A$1:$D$24   Browse...

Cancel   < Back   Next >   Finish

17	PacNW	Media Edge Interactive	51,927	$1,415,957
18	Mountain South	Elite Software Sales	245,813	$6,435,590
19	NorCal	Computronics	151,249	$3,489,469
20	NorCal	Powertech	453,918	$15,716,318
21	Mountain South	Falcon Retail	104,311	$2,822,940
22	SoCal	Falcon Retail	76,194	$1,361,030
23	SoCal	Ace Computer	226,487	$4,147,135
24	PacNW	Ace Computer	21,313	$382,389

Always make sure the range Excel suggests matches what you want. You can see we have all the data as well as the column headers in row 1 included in the range.

Next you have to tell Excel where to put the PivotTable. Excel defaults to putting it on a new worksheet because it's cleaner but you could specify somewhere in the existing workbook if you like.

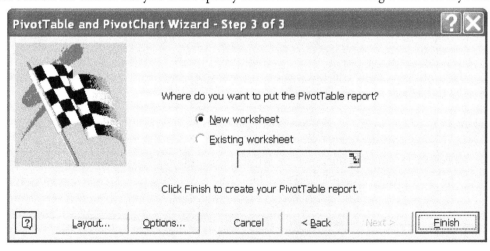

From here we hit Finish and Excel inserts a new sheet into the workbook with the following:

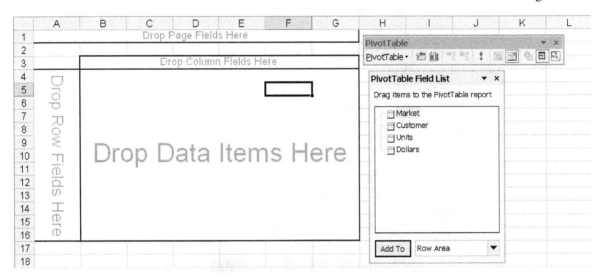

Notice that the selected cell above is F5 which happens to be in the default PivotTable layout. In this case, the default layout is the range A3:G16. Selecting any cell outside that range (even in A1:G2 which looks like it should be a part of the layout) yields the following:

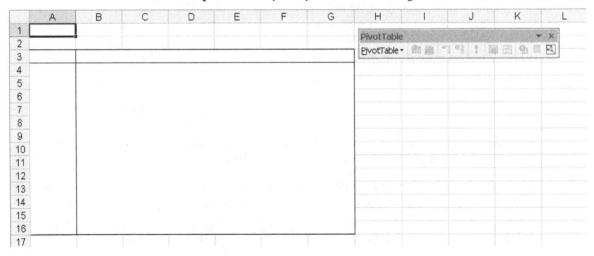

Notice that the PivotTable Field List has disappeared. To create the PivotTable we actually have to select in the default layout so let's go back to that.

Example 1

Suppose we want a report that tells us the total Dollars for each Customer by Market. In other words, we want Customers going down the left column (column A in this case) and have Markets going along the top row (row 3 in this case). Here's what we do:

1. Drag and drop the Market field form the PivotTable Field List on the right over to where it says "Drop Column Fields Here."

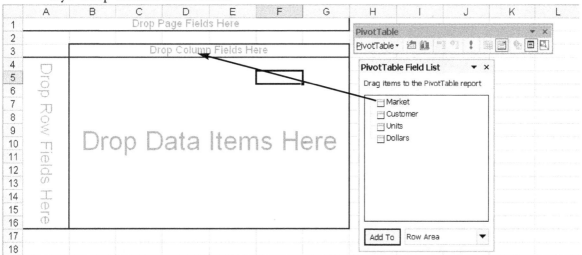

Our PivotTable will look like:

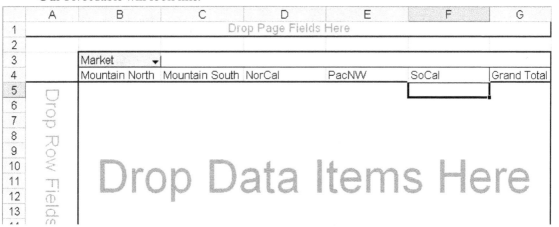

2. Drag and drop the Customer field from the PivotTable Field List on the right over to where it says "Drop Row Fields Here."

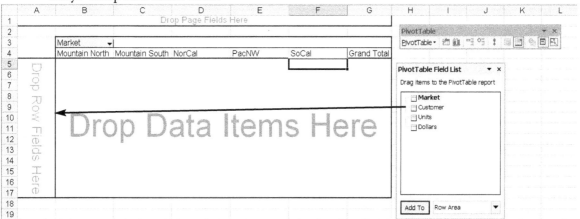

Our PivotTable will look like:

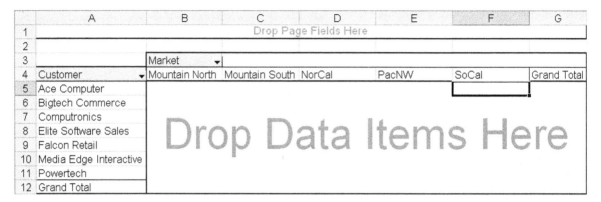

3. Drag and drop the Dollars field from the PivotTable Field List on the right over to where it says "Drop Data Items Here."

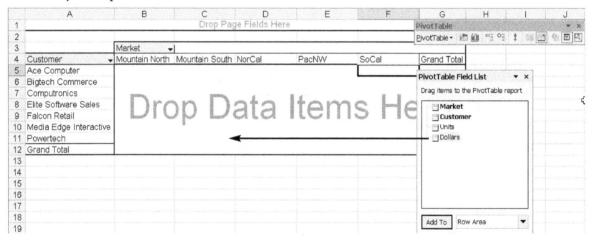

Our PivotTable will look like:

Count of Dollars	Market					
Customer	Mountain North	Mountain South	NorCal	PacNW	SoCal	Grand Total
Ace Computer	1		1	1	1	4
Bigtech Commerce		1	1		1	3
Computronics	1		1	1	1	4
Elite Software Sales		1	1			2
Falcon Retail		1	1	1	1	4
Media Edge Interactive			1	1	1	3
Powertech	1		1		1	3
Grand Total	3	3	7	4	6	23

In cell A3 in the image above, the PivotTable has defaulted to displaying the Count of occurrences of Dollars for Customers by Markets. We want the Sum of Dollars, so right click on cell A3 and select Field Settings from the dialog box. This brings up the following:

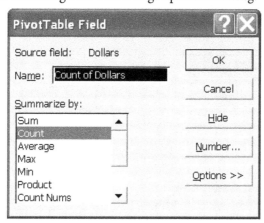

Simply chose Sum from the list and hit OK. The result is as follows:

	A	B	C	D	E	F	G
1			Drop Page Fields Here				
2							
3	Sum of Dollars	Market					
4	Customer	Mountain North	Mountain South	NorCal	PacNW	SoCal	Grand Total
5	Ace Computer	3209606		12884898	382389	4147135	20624028
6	Bigtech Commerce		1333535	754531		656161	2744227
7	Computronics	2152708		3489469	4269	11907492	17553938
8	Elite Software Sales		6435590	17441987			23877577
9	Falcon Retail		2822940	34362575	2226903	1361030	40773448
10	Media Edge Interactive			5085029	1415957	22075	6523061
11	Powertech	2370469		15716318		91802184	109888971
12	Grand Total	7732783	10592065	89734807	4029518	109896077	221985250

From here, we can copy and paste the values from the table somewhere else, apply formatting or do other things to the data to make it more presentable. For now, just recall the drag and drop nature of PivotTables:

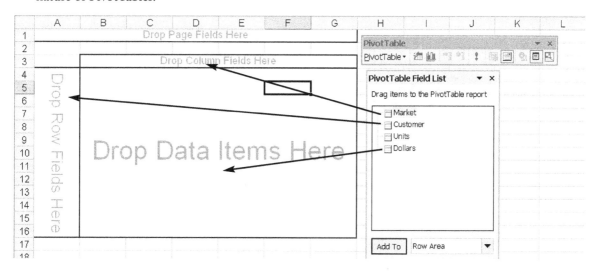

Example 2

Now suppose we want to see total Units and Dollars for each Market. To change the table we click on the Fields in the table and drag them outside the table to get rid of them. This means the following for our table:

	A	B	C	D	E	F	G
1			Drop Page Fields Here				
2							
3	Sum of Dollars	Market ▾					
4	Customer ▾	Mountain North	Mountain South	NorCal	PacNW	SoCal	Grand Total
5	Ace Computer	3209606		12884898	382389	4147135	20624028
6	Bigtech Commerce		1333535	754531		656161	2744227
7	Computronics	2152708		3489469	4269	11907492	17553938
8	Elite Software Sales		6435590	17441987			23877577
9	Falcon Retail		2822940	34362575	2226903	1361030	40773448
10	Media Edge Interactive			5085029	1415957	22075	6523061
11	Powertech	2370469		15716318		91802184	109888971
12	Grand Total	7732783	10592065	89734807	4029518	109896077	221985250

Click on the grey "button" in cell **A3** and drag it outside the table and let go to get rid of Sum of Dollars. Do the same for the "buttons" in **B3** and **A4**.

To create our new table, do the following:

1. Drag Market into the Row Fields area.
2. Drag Dollars into the Data Items area. For now, notice this gives the table shown at right.

	A	B
1	Drop Page Fields Here	
2		
3	Sum of Dollars	
4	Market ▾	Total
5	Mountain North	7732783
6	Mountain South	10592065
7	NorCal	89734807
8	PacNW	4029518
9	SoCal	109896077

3. Now drag Units into the Data Items area (in this case, somewhere in **B4:B10**) and we'll see the following:

	A	B	C
1		Drop Page Fields Here	
2			
3	Market ▾	Data ▾	Total
4	Mountain North	Sum of Dollars	7732783
5		Sum of Units	275722
6	Mountain South	Sum of Dollars	10592065
7		Sum of Units	401709
8	NorCal	Sum of Dollars	89734807
9		Sum of Units	3240415
10	PacNW	Sum of Dollars	4029518
11		Sum of Units	149117
12	SoCal	Sum of Dollars	109896077
13		Sum of Units	3505486
14	Total Sum of Dollars		221985250
15	Total Sum of Units		7572449

4. Notice that this isn't quite what we want. We want Units and Dollars along the top and not nested within each Market as shown at left. To fix this, click on the "button" in **B3** (where it says Data) and drag it into cell **C3** where it says Total:

	A	B	C
1		Drop Page Fields Here	
2			
3		Data ▾	
4	Market ▾	Sum of Dollars	Sum of Units
5	Mountain North	7732783	275722
6	Mountain South	10592065	401709
7	NorCal	89734807	3240415
8	PacNW	4029518	149117
9	SoCal	109896077	3505486
10	Grand Total	221985250	7572449

Find/Replace

This is a very simple but often overlooked feature, especially when doing data processing. Usually people think of Find/Replace as something one would use in a Word document or presentation, but in Excel it is just as powerful, if not *more*.

Two key features of Find/Replace:

- If you have only <u>one cell selected</u> when you execute a Find/Replace, Excel will execute the Find/Replace <u>on the entire sheet</u>.
- If a <u>range is highlighted</u> when you execute a Find/Replace, Excel will execute the Find/Replace <u>on just the range</u>.

Use Ctrl+F to open Find. Note the Options button:

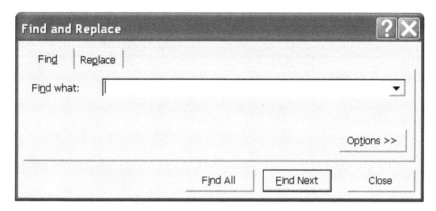

Clicking on Options expands the dialog box:

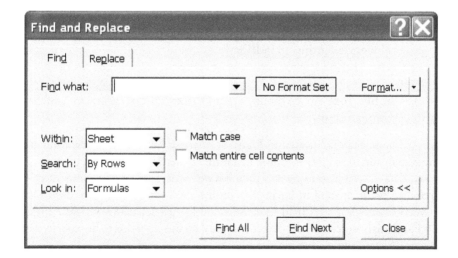

Clicking on the Replace tab shows the following:

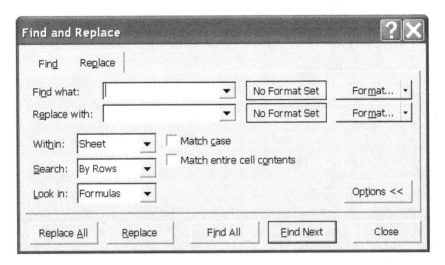

Notice that you can click on the Replace tab in the same dialog box. You could also have hit Ctrl+H to get to replace directly.

- Use Ctrl+F to open Find.
- Use Ctrl+H to open Replace.

Using Find/Replace is straight forward but keep in mind that you must be aware of the options you are setting. Note that you can specify case sensitivity and whether you want to search for entire cells of the find criteria.

Note:
Watch out for a bug on doing Find/Replace on ranges with formulas in the cells. This is where we would quickly copy and paste values of the range (by selecting the range, hitting Ctrl+C and then Alt–E–S–V–Enter) before executing a Find/Replace.

Text to Columns

(This lesson uses the files Text to Columns.xls and Text to Columns.txt which are available at www.excelbreakthrough.com.)

Every corporate financial and data analyst I have ever worked with has had to deal with data coming from one system and massaging it for use in another system or for another purpose. They receive text files or raw data dumps into Excel and then have to process the data in some way. Often when such a source data file is opened in Excel the column delineators may have been lost. Each row might be treated as one long text field that the analyst must somehow separate into columns as intended. Or Excel might automatically detect that the data was intended to be separated into columns and try to separate them upon opening the file.

The image below shows a text file of data that is typical of output from a database.

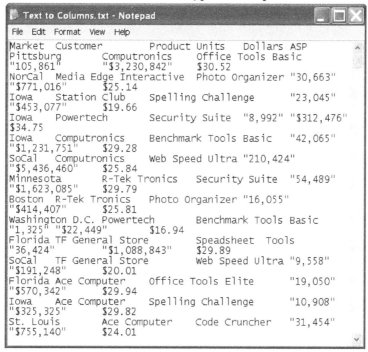

The file is Word Wrapped for ease of displaying here, but look at the first line of text in the file closely. Notice it reads:

Market   Customer   Product   Units   Dollars   ASP

Those fields are actually column headers. Like many text files, this one is delimited by Tabs, meaning in each column the data fields are separated by Tabs. If we use Excel to open this file here is what we see:

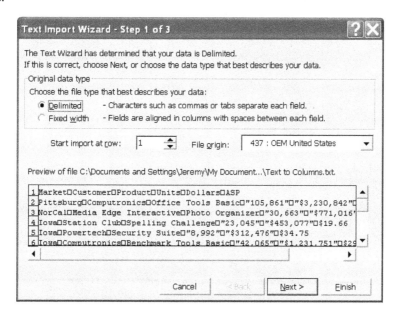

Excel is smart enough to interpret a text file and even guess at how it was intended to be displayed in rows and columns. Thus, Excel opened the Text Import Wizard which is the same thing as the Covert Text to Column Wizard which we will cover in a moment.

In this case, we see that the Delimited option is checked when we open it so we simply hit the Next button to get to step two:

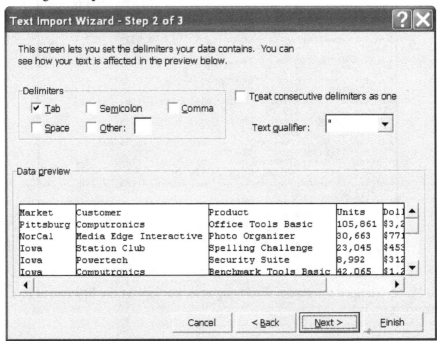

Notice in the image above that by default Excel has detected a Tab-delimited file. In the Data preview area we see how Excel will split the columns. This looks right so we hit Next to go to step 3:

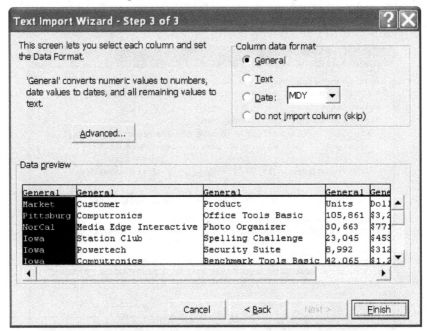

Here you can tweak the format of each column by selecting it with the mouse in the <u>Data pre-view</u> area and then selecting from the options in the <u>Column data format</u> area in the upper right. In this case, we simply hit the Finish button. Here is the result in Excel:

	A	B	C	D	E	F
1	Market	Customer	Product	Units	Dollars	ASP
2	Pittsburg	Computror	Office Too	105,861	$3,230,842	$30.52
3	NorCal	Media Edg	Photo Org	30,663	$771,016	$25.14
4	Iowa	Station Clu	Spelling Cl	23,045	$453,077	$19.66
5	Iowa	Powertech	Security S	8,992	$312,476	$34.75
6	Iowa	Computror	Benchmar	42,065	$1,231,751	$29.28
7	SoCal	Computror	Web Spee	210,424	$5,436,460	$25.84
8	Minnesota	R-Tek Tror	Security S	54,489	$1,623,085	$29.79
9	Boston	R-Tek Tror	Photo Org	16,055	$414,407	$25.81
10	Washingtc	Powertech	Benchmar	1,325	$22,449	$16.94
11	Florida	TF Genera	Speadshee	36,424	$1,088,843	$29.89
12	SoCal	TF Genera	Web Spee	0,558	$101,248	$20.01

The image above only shows the beginning rows of the entire data set but the import is raw with no formatting applied beyond the simple number formats that were in the source text file. Even the column widths have not been adjusted.

A few things to keep in mind:

- Excel can import almost any type of text file regardless if it is delimited by tabs, spaces, commas, semi-colons, quotation marks or other specified characters.
- Most text files are tab or comma delimited.
  - Tab delimited text files have .txt file extensions, such as `Text to Columns.txt`
  - Comma delimited text files have .csv file extensions, such as `Text to Columns.csv`
- When importing text files, you may have to play around with the options in the Text Import Wizard to get it to look right once it's finally imported into Excel.

Convert Text to Columns Wizard

(This lesson uses the files `Text to Columns.xls` and `Text to Columns.txt` which are available at www.excelbreakthrough.com.)

Now suppose that we have a column of text as in the picture at right.

Notice that each row has a single text string in column A. Further, we can see that the first word in each string is a Color, the second is a Size and the third is a Style. Our task is to separate these text strings in column A into distinct text fields that populate columns A, B, and C, and to do so we will use the Convert Text to Columns Wizard.

Here's what we do:

1.   Select A1.

	A	B
1	Color Size Style	
2	Green Large A	
3	Red Large B	
4	Blue Small B	
5	Yellow Medium A	
6	Blue Medium A	
7	Green Small A	
8	Blue Large B	
9	Red Medium B	
10	Red Medium B	
11	Green Large A	
12	Blue Small A	

e

2. Ctrl+Spacebar to select all of column A.

    a. Like the Sort feature, we need to tell Excel what text we want
        to convert to columns so the Wizard knows what to do.

    b. Unlike the Sort feature, Covert Text to Columns will not
        auto detect your entire data column, so we need to select our
        entire set of data <u>first</u>.

3. Alt–D–E to open the Convert Text to Columns Wizard.

4. In Step 1 of the wizard, make sure Delimited is selected.

    a. Hit Next to go to Step 2.

5. In Step 2, select Space from the Delimiters list if Excel has not
    detected Space as the delimiter type already.

    a. This can be done by hitting the S key because it is a hotkey
        for Space in the wizard as show below.

    b. Notice below that leaving Tab selected has no impact because in this case the data is
        actually delimited by Spaces.

    c. Also notice below that in the Data preview area we can see how text strings will be split
        into columns.

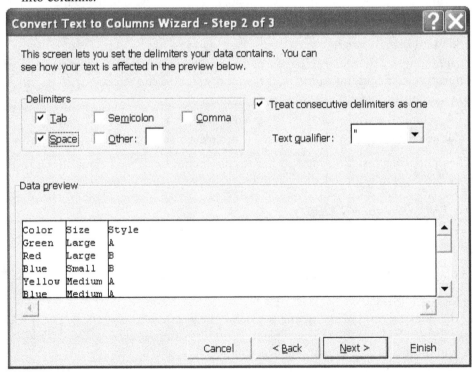

6. Hit Next to get to Step 3:

    a. Here you can change data formats of any column. In this case, as with most data sets,
        you probably won't need to do anything. It is most often used when you need to
        change a number format on a column.

b. You can also set the desired location of where to dump the parsed columns on the worksheet in the Destination select box. This is sometimes important because you might want to save the original column. If you leave the Destination cell set to the upper left corner cell of the column you are splitting, the Wizard will over write that that column automatically, which is often what you want to do anyway.

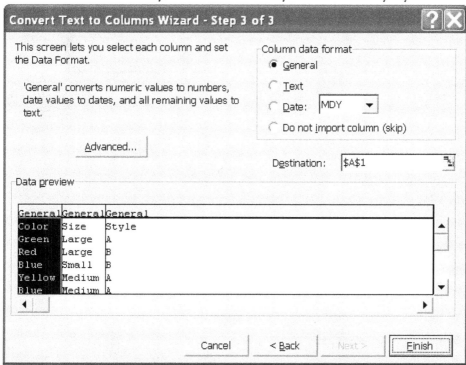

7. Hit Finish to see our end product at right.

	A	B	C
1	Color	Size	Style
2	Green	Large	A
3	Red	Large	B
4	Blue	Small	B
5	Yellow	Medium	A
6	Blue	Medium	A
7	Green	Small	A
8	Blue	Large	B

A Slight Variation on the Above Example

Suppose we have the exact same situation except that we have some non-empty cells in columns B and C as shown at right.

	A	B	C
1	Color Size	Total Units	Total Cost
2	Green Lar	35	$420
3	Red Large B		
4	Blue Small B		
5	Yellow Medium A		
6	Blue Medium A		
7	Green Small A		
8	Blue Large B		

If we go through the exact same sequence of converting the text strings in column A to parsed columns in A, B and C, the wizard will give us the following warning:

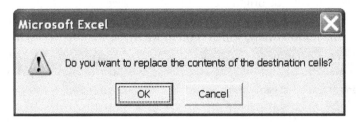

This is actually a nice feature of the wizard because it double checks if we want to overwrite these cells or not.

Lesson 7 – Formulas

Like some Excel features such as Sort or PivotTables, we could dedicate an entire book to cell formulas alone. Although there are many formulas we can use, here we will focus on essential constructs that use formulas to help you process data efficiently.

Remember that cell formulas are the primary benefit of spreadsheet applications. The ability to store data in one visual location on the screen (i.e., in a cell or in multiple cells in a range) and then do calculations or logical operations based on such cell value(s) was a breakthrough that changed personal computing. Without computer spreadsheets, think how difficult it would be to do any kind of financial analysis where the inputs change or require multiple iterations and sensitivity analysis. With a spreadsheet you can store all the data right in front of you and calculate just about anything you need and save it in a file so you can come back to it later or share it. Without spreadsheets we would still be using pen, paper and calculators. Anyone who does financial analysis on a computer will tell you that Excel is as fundamental a tool as a hammer is to a carpenter.

Here's what's coming in this lesson on formulas:

- What Is the Purpose of Formulas?
- Formula Basics
- The Formula Bar
- F2
- The Core Formulas You Need to Know
  - IF
  - Nested IF
  - EXACT
  - VLOOKUP
  - HLOOKUP
  - MAX
  - MIN
  - LEFT
  - RIGHT
  - MID
  - PROPER
  - UPPER & LOWER
  - TRIM
  - FIND
  - SUMIF
  - COUNTIF
  - AMPERSAND (&)
- Relative and Absolute Cell References
- F4
- Nested Formulas

What Is the Purpose of Formulas?

Formulas capture logical thought energy in our brains and record them so we only have to think the logic once. For most of us, it takes time to sum 5 different numbers in our heads or even with a calculator. But Excel can do it instantly.

Formulas might give us answers to questions such as:

- What is the sum of a set of numbers?
- What is the average age of people on a list?
- What is the median income across the counties of New York?
- What is the Present Value of a set of cash flows?

Formula Basics

Most people who use Excel know the fundamental logic of all cell formulas:

- Put a formula in one cell that has its inputs from other cells. You can put constants in a formula but usually people don't.

The most basic formulas people know in Excel essentially mimic how we use a calculator. These include:

- Add/Subtract/Multiply/Divide
- Sum

Up to this point we have seen examples of these and you will see them again in Part 3, so we're going to skip past these basic formulas and get to less common ones that are critical to having an *Excel Breakthrough*. These are the formulas you need to know.

The Formula Bar

Under the View menu is an option to display or hide the Formula Bar.

Enabling the Formula Bar allows us to see what formula is in the selected cell. I always have the Formula Bar visible. Below you can see the Formula Bar where it reads:

=A1+B1

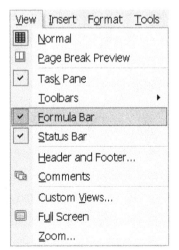

Also notice the Insert Function button next to where the formula in cell C1 is displayed. It looks like f_x. Clicking that will bring up the Insert Function dialog box:

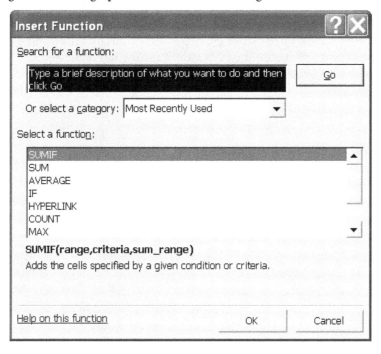

Spend time looking through this dialog box as much as you can. It provides detailed information, help and examples on every formula in Excel. Formulas are grouped into Categories as shown in the dropdown menu:

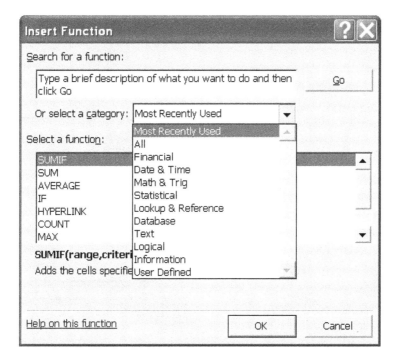

F2

(This lesson uses the file `F2.xls` available at www.excelbreakthrough.com.)

If you want to edit the contents of a cell that already has a formula in it, you normally have to use the mouse to double click on it, or select the cell and edit the contents in the Formula Bar. The faster way is to select the cell and hit the F2 button along the top of the keyboard. It saves a lot of time when your mind is in keyboard mode. This is also a good opportunity for another preview of the kinds of examples from Part 3 of this book that tie a few lessons from Part 2 together.

Consider the "F2 Before" tab from the file `F2.xls` showing the calculation of a total bill on the sale of an item. Suppose we were modeling the bill at a restaurant and wanted to add a line for the tip. To do this without the mouse, we could do the following:

1. Starting with B3 as the selected cell, hit Shift+Space to highlight row 3:

B3		▾	*fx* =B1+B1*B2
	A	B	C
1	Sales Amount	$100	
2	Tax Rate	8%	
3	Total Bill	$108	

2. Then hit the Menu button...

B3		▾	*fx* =B1+B1*B2
	A	B	C
1	Sales Amount	$100	
2	Tax Rate	8%	
3	Total Bill	$108	
4	✂ Cut		
5	🗐 Copy		
6	📋 Paste		
7	Paste Special...		
8	Insert		
9	Delete		

3. Then hit I to insert a row between rows 2 and 3.

	A	B	C
1	Sales Amount	$100	
2	Tax Rate	8%	
3			
4	Total Bill	$108	
5			

4. Hit Left to select A3.

	A	B	C
1	Sales Amount	$100	
2	Tax Rate	8%	
3			
4	Total Bill	$108	
5			

5. Enter the word "Tip" into A3.
6. Key over to cell **B4** and hit the F2 button.

	A	B	C
SUMIF		▾ ✕ ✓ *fx* =B1+B1*B2	
1	Sales Amount	$100	
2	Tax Rate	8%	
3	Tip		
4	Total Bill	=B1+B1*B2	
5			

7. Now you will be editing the formula directly in **B4**. After where it says "B2" type "+**B3**" so that it looks like this:

	A	B	C
SUMIF		▾ ✕ ✓ *fx* =B1+B1*B2+b3	
1	Sales Amount	$100	
2	Tax Rate	8%	
3	Tip		
4	Total Bill	=B1+B1*B2+b3	
5			

8. Hit Enter and the formula is complete.
9. Now go back to **B3** and enter any amount. In this case I put 10 for $10. Notice the format in **B3** is the same as the format in **B2** because I inserted a blank row between rows 2 and 3 earlier. The new row picked up the formatting of the row above it as shown at right.

	A	B	C
B3		▾ *fx* 10%	
1	Sales Amount	$100	
2	Tax Rate	8%	
3	Tip	10%	
4	Total Bill	$108	

10. With **B3** selected, hit Menu–F to bring up the Format Cells dialog box. Select the Number tab if it isn't already selected and then select Currency and hit Enter.

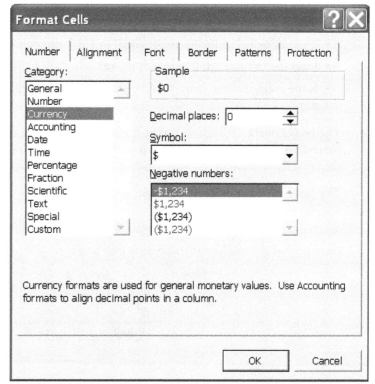

11. Now notice the value in B3 is 0.1. This is because when we entered the value 10 in that cell originally, the format was set to Percentage and Excel interpreted it as 10% which is 0.l when unformatted. This is a bit confusing to Excel beginners. All we do is type in the value 10 and hit Enter to get the result shown at right.

B3		▼	fx	10
	A		B	C
1	Sales Amount		$100	
2	Tax Rate		8%	
3	Tip		$10	
4	Total Bill		$118	
5				

That's a long example, but it puts F2 in the right context.

Bonus note:

F2 works in Windows similar to how it works in Excel. If you want to rename a file, select the file in Explorer, hit F2 and you'll be able to retype the name.

The Core Formulas You Need to Know

(This lesson uses the file Formulas.xls available at www.excelbreakthrough.com.)

IF

This is the most important formula for the purpose of having an *Excel Breakthrough*. When you want to organize data, you need to make decisions about each data point. What's great about computers on a fundamental level, and even in life, is that ultimately things either *are* something or they *are not*. In Excel, consider these simple examples:

- Does the text in cell A1 contain the sequence "RED" in it or not? It either does or it does not.
- Is the value in cell B5 greater or equal to 10? It either is or it is not.
- Does the value in cell C20 match the value in C19? It either does or it does not.
- Is the average of the range A1:A5 equal to the difference between B5 and B4? It either is or is not.

The power of the IF formula is that it allows us to process data in new ways that helps us make faster decisions and avoid huge amounts of manual processing, particularly when we need to apply the same mini-decision to a thousand cells in a table, one at a time.

The Basic structure of the IF function is as follows:

=IF(logical_test, value_if_true, value_if_false)

Here is what it looks like as you type it into a cell:

SUMIF		▼ X ✓ fx	=if(		
	A	B	C	D	E
1	100	=if(			
2		IF(**logical_test**, [value_if_true], [value_if_false])			
3					

The logical_test is something that is either TRUE or FALSE. Excel checks the logical test and if the result is TRUE, then the formula will yield whatever is in the value_if_true field. If the result is FALSE, then the formula will yield whatever is in the value_if_false field.

In the above image, suppose we set this as the formula:

SUMIF		▾ ✕ ✓ *fx* =if(A1>50,"Green","Red")		
	A	B	C	D	E
1	100	=if(A1>50,"Green","Red")			
2		IF(logical_test, [value_if_true], **[value_if_false]**)			
3					

The result would be:

B1		▾	*fx* =IF(A1>50,"Green","Red")		
	A	B	C	D	E
1	100	Green			
2					

In this case, we set the value_if_true and value_if_false fields set to show text. We could input a number, or we could even put a reference to another cell. If we leave the value_if_false field blank, the result would simply be 0, such as in the example below.

B1		▾	*fx* =IF(A1>150,"Green",)		
	A	B	C	D	E
1	100	0			
2					

There are many more examples to show you, however the use of them in the context of *Excel Breakthrough* will really be shown in Part 3. The IF formula is very handy for picking items from a long list of data cells that meet specific criteria.

Nested IF
Sometimes you need to check one criterion for being True or False, then based on the result check another criterion for being True or False. In Excel, this means using an IF formula within another IF formula.

In simple terms, it might look like this.

C1		▾	*fx* =IF(A1>50,IF(B1<300,"Green","Red"),"Blue")			
	A	B	C	D	E	F	G
1	100	200	Green				
2							

If you are unfamiliar with the Nested IF, then this may seem hard to read but it's not complicated. The logic of the formula in the above picture is as follows:

If A1 is greater than 50, and if B1 is less than 300, then in C1 put "Green" ... but if B1 is not less than 300, then in C1 put "Red" ... but if A1 was not greater than 50 in the first place, then in C1 put "Blue."

That's a long and messy way of saying it, but often when working with complex data sets I use Nested IF formulas to model the actual logic to extract the data I need.

EXACT

The EXACT formula checks whether two text strings are exactly the same, and returns TRUE or FALSE. EXACT is case sensitive. This is very simple to use. You can check the text value in one cell against the text value in another cell. The two images at right illustrate just how easy it is:

B1		f_x =EXACT(A1,C1)		
A	B	C	D	E
1 Green	TRUE	Green		
2 Blue	FALSE	Red		

B2		f_x =EXACT(A2,C2)		
A	B	C	D	E
1 Green	TRUE	Green		
2 Blue	FALSE	Red		

VLOOKUP

VLOOKUP checks for a value in the leftmost column of a table, then returns a value in the same row from a column you specify. That may sound odd, but it's very powerful and can save a huge amount of time. I use VLOOKUP frequently and some of the biggest time saving examples in Part 3 use it as the central method.

The syntax for VLOOKUP is as follows:

=VLOOKUP(lookup_value,table_array,col_index,range_lookup)

- **lookup_value** is the value to find in the first column of a table_array.
- **table_array** is a table of two or more columns of data. (Yes, it's really that simple: just a table of data with two or more columns.)
- **col_index** is the column number in the table_array from which the matching value should be returned. The first column of values in the table is column 1.
  - To have VLOOKUP return values from the second column, set col_index to 2. To return values from the third column, set col_index to 3. Etc.
  - This is always a positive integer. Only enter positive integers or the formula will return the #VALUE! error.
  - If you set the col_index to a number that is greater than the number of columns in the table, the formula will return the #REF! error.
- **range_lookup** determines if you are looking for an exact match based on the lookup_value. If you enter TRUE, the formula will return an approximate match, which means that if no exact match is found the formula will return the next largest value that is less than the lookup_value. If you enter FALSE the formula will look for an exact match and if it does not find one it will return #N/A.

Example

Suppose we have the two tables shown below:

	A	B	C	D	E	F	G
1	Product	Class	User Rating	ASP		Product	ASP
2	Benchmark Tools Pro	Tech	88%			Ad-Spy Defense	$16.63
3	Office Tools Basic	Office	84%			Audit Deluxe	$15.17
4	Photo Organizer	Creative	86%			Audit Pro	$20.22
5	Speadsheet Tools	Office	95%			Benchmark Tools Pro	$25.19
6	Web Speed Ultra	Tech	91%			Browser Central	$29.42
7	Disk Suite	Tech	95%			Office Tools Basic	$34.96
8						Office Tools Elite	$34.16
9						Photo Organizer	$30.91
10						Productivity Bundle	$24.82
11						Security Suite	$22.01
12						Speadsheet Tools	$26.26
13						Web Speed Ultra	$25.58

The first table is in range A1:D7 and the second table is in the range F1:G13. Suppose we want to look up the ASP of each product in the fist table from the second table. We could very easily do this manually because there are only six pieces of information to look up, and the table on the left isn't much larger. Remember, what if you had to look up the ASP of 600 products from a table of 6,000 total products? This example illustrates how VLOOKUP can save us time.

To quickly fill in the ASP column of the first table using VLOOKUP, we do the following:

1. Select D2 and manually type **=vlookup(** and notice how Excel prompts us for the inputs:

SUMIF		▾ ✕ ✓ *fx* =vlookup(						
	A	B	C	D	E	F	G	H
1	Product	Class	User Rating	ASP		Product	ASP	
2	Benchmark Tools Pro	Tech	88%	=vlookup(		Ad-Spy Defense	$16.63	
3	Office Tools Basic	Office	84%	VLOOKUP(**lookup_value**, table_array, col_index_num, [range_lookup])				

2. To enter the **lookup_value**, we'll use the Left key (or Ctrl+Left) to select A2:

SUMIF		▾ ✕ ✓ *fx* =vlookup(A2				
	A	B	C	D	E	
1	Product	Class	User Rating	ASP		Pr
2	Benchmark Tools Pro	Tech	88%	=vlookup(A2		Ad-
3	Office Tools Basic	Office	84%	VLOOKUP(**lookup_value**,		
4	Photo Organizer	Creative	86%			Au

3. Then hit comma and Excel prompts for the **table_array**:

SUMIF		▾ ✕ ✓ *fx* =vlookup(A2,						
	A	B	C	D	E	F	G	H
1	Product	Class	User Rating	ASP		Product	ASP	
2	Benchmark Tools Pro	Tech	88%	=vlookup(A2,		Ad-Spy Defense	$16.63	
3	Office Tools Basic	Office	84%	VLOOKUP(lookup_value, **table_array**, col_index_num, [range_lookup])				
4	Photo Organizer	Creative	86%			Audit Pro	$20.22	

4. Next we select columns F through G. We can do that with the mouse or the keyboard:
   a. Hit Right to move over to F2.
   b. Ctrl+Spacebar to select column F.
   c. Shift+Right to select F:G.

The result is:

	SUMIF	▾	X ✓ *fx*	=vlookup(A2,F:G				
	A	B	C	D	E	F	G	H
1	Product	Class	User Rating	ASP		Product	ASP	
2	Benchmark Tools Pro	Tech	88%	=vlookup(A2,F:G		Ad-Spy Defense	$16.63	
3	Office Tools Basic	Office	84%	VLOOKUP(lookup_value, **table_array**, col_index_num, [range_lookup])				
4	Photo Organizer	Creative	86%			Audit Pro	$20.22	
5	Speadsheet Tools	Office	95%			Benchmark Tools Pro	$25.19	
6	Web Speed Ultra	Tech	91%			Browser Central	$29.42	
7	Disk Suite	Tech	95%			Office Tools Basic	$34.96	
8						Office Tools Elite	$34.16	
9						Photo Organizer	$30.91	
10						Productivity Bundle	$24.82	
11						Security Suite	$22.01	
12						Speadsheet Tools	$26.26	
13						Web Speed Ultra	$25.58	

5. Next we enter the last two parameters:
   a. Set col_index_num to 2.
   b. Set [range_lookup] to FALSE. Just type in the word "false" and it works.
   c. Hit Enter to finish the formula.

At this point our formula in B2 looks like:

	D2	▾		*fx*	=VLOOKUP(A2,F:G,2,FALSE)		
	A	B	C	D	E	F	G
1	Product	Class	User Rating	ASP		Product	ASP
2	Benchmark Tools Pro	Tech	88%	$25.19		Ad-Spy Defense	$16.63
3	Office Tools Basic	Office	84%			Audit Deluxe	$15.17
4	Photo Organizer	Creative	86%			Audit Pro	$20.22
5	Speadsheet Tools	Office	95%			Benchmark Tools Pro	$25.19
6	Web Speed Ultra	Tech	91%			Browser Central	$29.42
7	Disk Suite	Tech	95%			Office Tools Basic	$34.96
8						Office Tools Elite	$34.16
9						Photo Organizer	$30.91
10						Productivity Bundle	$24.82
11						Security Suite	$22.01
12						Speadsheet Tools	$26.26
13						Web Speed Ultra	$25.58

6. Finally, we use Control Method to highlight the range D2:D7 and Fill down. Starting from D2 as the selected cell, do the following:
   a. Left to select C2.
   b. Ctrl+Down to select C7.
   c. Right to select D7.

d. Ctrl+Shift+Up to select D2:D7.

e. Ctrl+D to Fill down the formulas.

The final result looks as follows:

D7   ▼   *fx* =VLOOKUP(A7,F:G,2,FALSE)

	A	B	C	D	E	F	G
1	Product	Class	User Rating	ASP		Product	ASP
2	Benchmark Tools Pro	Tech	88%	$25.19		Ad-Spy Defense	$16.63
3	Office Tools Basic	Office	84%	$34.96		Audit Deluxe	$15.17
4	Photo Organizer	Creative	86%	$30.91		Audit Pro	$20.22
5	Speadsheet Tools	Office	95%	$26.26		Benchmark Tools Pro	$25.19
6	Web Speed Ultra	Tech	91%	$25.58		Browser Central	$29.42
7	Disk Suite	Tech	95%	#N/A		Office Tools Basic	$34.96
8						Office Tools Elite	$34.16
9						Photo Organizer	$30.91
10						Productivity Bundle	$24.82
11						Security Suite	$22.01
12						Speadsheet Tools	$26.26
13						Web Speed Ultra	$25.58

Notice that D7 shows #N/A because the product "Disk Suite" does not appear in the second table on the right. If we had set the [range_lookup] of the formula to TRUE instead of FALSE, the formula in D7 would have returned $29.42 because "Disk Suite" would fall directly below "Browser Central" if it *had* been in the second table. In this case, the formula picks up the value from "Browser Central" and uses that for the result in D7.

HLOOKUP

HLOOKUP is just like VLOOKUP except it works with the rows of a table_array instead of the columns. I hardly ever use this formula as almost all of the time I work data in columns. If you ever need to use HLOOKUP, make sure you know how to use VLOOKUP first and then the logic for using HLOOKUP will flow easily. But again, because this is used with much less frequency we can skip it.

MAX

MAX is like the SUM formula except instead of summing the inputs, it simply returns the maximum value of the inputs.

B1 ▼ *fx* =MAX(A1:A5)

	A	B	C	D
1	1	5	1	
2	2			
3	3			
4	4			
5	5			

MIN

MIN is also like the SUM formula except instead of summing the inputs, it simply returns the minimum value of the inputs.

C1 ▼ *fx* =MIN(A1:A5)

	A	B	C	D
1	1	5	1	
2	2			
3	3			
4	4			
5	5			

LEFT

LEFT allows you to pull a specified number of the leftmost characters from a text string in another cell that you specify. The syntax is:

$$=LEFT(string, number\_of\_characters)$$

In the table below, the formulas on the left would return the results at the right.

	B1	▼	f_x =LEFT(A1,3)

	A	B	C
1	XRT 1159	XRT	
2	BNG 1285		
3	KFO 9927		
4	VQL 1436		

Formula:	Result:
= LEFT(A1, 5)	"XRT 1"
= LEFT(A2, 3)	"BNG"

Also, if for some reason you put a string in the formula it would function the same. Thus the following formula ...

$$=LEFT("Excel\ Breakthrough", 5)$$

... returns "Excel" and nothing else.

RIGHT

RIGHT allows you to pull a specified number of the rightmost characters from a text string in another cell that you specify. The syntax is:

$$=RIGHT(string, number\_of\_characters)$$

In the table below, the formulas on the left would return the results at the right.

	B2	▼	f_x =RIGHT(A2,4)

	A	B	C
1	XRT 1159	XRT	
2	BNG 1285	1285	
3	KFO 9927		
4	VQL 1436		

Formula:	Result:
= RIGHT(A2, 5)	" 1285"
= RIGHT(A3, 6)	"O 9927"

Also, if for some reason you put a string in the formula it would function the same. Thus following formula ...

$$=Right("Excel\ Breakthrough", 7)$$

... returns "through" and nothing else.

The LEFT and RIGHT formulas may seem a bit obscure if you have never thought to use them, but I find I use them *nearly every day* when I'm helping clients with Excel analyses.

MID

MID is similar to RIGHT and LEFT in that it allows you to extract a specified number of characters from a text string but unlike LEFT or RIGHT you can specify the exact starting place of the number of characters you want to extract.

The syntax is:

=MID(*string*, starting_character, number_of_characters)

B3		▼	*fx* =MID(A3,3,4)	
	A		B	C
1	XRT 1159		XRT	
2	BNG 1285		1285	
3	KFO 9927		O 99	
4	VQL 1436			

The way to read the formula =MID(A3,3,4) is:

> *From the text in cell **A3**, start with the third character and extract 4 characters from left to right, starting with that character.*

So Excel looks at the text in A3 and counts over three characters: K, F, and O. Thus, it starts with O and extracts it plus the next three characters for a total of four characters. Remember that spaces are characters! This explains why =MID(A3,3,4) returns "O 99" as shown above.

PROPER

PROPER simply capitalizes the first character in each word of a string and makes all the other characters in each word lower case.

The syntax is:

=PROPER(*string*)

B6		▼	*fx* =PROPER(A6)	
	A		B	C
5				
6	EXCEL		Excel	
7	BREAKTHROUGH		Breakthrough	
8	TOAster		Toaster	
9	computer printer		Computer Printer	

Above, you can see what PROPER (A6) returns. Cells B7 through B9 have PROPER formulas in them using cells A7 through A9 as inputs, respectively.

UPPER & LOWER

UPPER capitalizes all the characters of a text string. LOWER makes all the characters lower case.

Here is an example of the UPPER formula:

B11		▼	*fx*	=UPPER(A11)

	A	B	C
10			
11	Excel	EXCEL	

Here is an example of the LOWER formula:

B12		▼	*fx*	=LOWER(A12)

	A	B	C
10			
11	Excel	EXCEL	
12	EXCEL	excel	
13			

TRIM

TRIM removes the leading and trailing spaces of a string. Pretend we typed " ABC 123 " into cell A13. We have three spaces before ABC and three spaces after 123. Here is what TRIM does:

B13		▼	*fx*	=TRIM(A13)

	A	B	C
11	Excel	EXCEL	
12	EXCEL	excel	
13	ABC 123	ABC 123	
14			

FIND (the formula)

Before you get confused, FIND is not just a function accessible from the Edit menu or by hitting Ctrl+F. FIND is also a text function that returns the starting position of one text string within another text string. (FIND is also case sensitive.)

The syntax is:

=FIND(find_text, within_text, start_num)

- **find_text** is the text you want to find. Use double quotes (empty text) to match the first character in within_text

- **within_text** is the text containing the text you want to find. Usually this means a cell reference as in the example below.

- **start_num** is an optional parameter. It specifies the character at which to start the search. The first character in within_text is the character number. If omitted, start_num = 1.

C13		▼	*fx*	=FIND("C",B13)

	A	B	C	D
11	Excel	EXCEL		
12	EXCEL	excel		
13	ABC 123	ABC 123	3	
14				

SUMIF

The SUMIF formula essentially combines the commonly known SUM formula and IF formula into one.

The syntax is:

=SUMIF(range,criteria,sum_range)

This is best explained by example. Suppose you have the range of cells shown at right.

If you wanted to know the sum of all cells in the table where the value is greater than 2, the formula would be:

=SUMIF(A1:A10,">2")

	A	B
1	1	
2	2	
3	4	
4	5	
5	3	
6	1	
7	2	
8	5	
9	1	
10	3	

B1   ▼   *fx* =SUMIF(A1:A10,">2")

	A	B	C	D	E
1	1	20			
2	2				
3	4				
4	5				
5	3				

Notice that our criteria have to be in quotes.

Also notice that SUMIF has three inputs and in the example formula above we have two. The sum_range input is optional. To explain, now consider the data at right.

Suppose we wanted to know the sum of values in column C that are in the same row as values in column A that are greater than two. In other words, we want to go down the range in column A and for each cell with a value greater than 2, add the value from the same row in column C. Here's how it's done:

G19   ▼   *fx*

	A	B	C
1	1		7,100
2	2		1,295
3	4		4,554
4	5		6,581
5	3		6,105
6	1		4,863
7	2		9,790
8	5		5,664
9	1		1,757
10	3		9,384

B1   ▼   *fx* =SUMIF(A1:A10,">2",C1:C10)

	A	B	C	D	E	F
1	1	32,288	7,100			
2	2		1,295			
3	4		4,554			
4	5		6,581			
5	3		6,105			
6	1		4,863			
7	2		9,790			
8	5		5,664			
9	1		1,757			
10	3		9,384			

This use of SUMIF isn't as common, but it does have its uses when trying to sum selected data from a list when you can't use a Filter.

COUNTIF

The COUNTIF formula essentially combines the commonly known COUNT formula and IF formula into one.

The syntax is:

=COUNTIF(range,criteria)

It works essentially the same as SUMIF except instead of yielding the sum it simply counts the number of occurrences the criteria is met in a range.

AMPERSAND (&)

The Ampersand symbol (found on the 7 key on most keyboards) can be used to concatenate[9] text, data, formula results and other values in cells into one string. It is very powerful when constructing long strings from many different inputs. It is really a feature of Excel formulas in general rather than a formula itself.

Examine the formula in cell **B14** in the following picture:

B14	▼	*fx* =B11&B12&B13	
	A	B	C
10			
11	Excel	EXCEL	
12	EXCEL	excel	
13	ABC 123	ABC 123	
14		EXCELexcelABC 123	

Now consider this modification to the formula in **B14**:

B14	▼	*fx* =B11&" "&B12&" "&B13	
	A	B	C
10			
11	Excel	EXCEL	
12	EXCEL	excel	
13	ABC 123	ABC 123	
14		EXCEL excel ABC 123	

Notice that to concatenate the text from **B11**, **B12** and **B13** with spaces, we needed to modify the formula from …

=B11&B12&B13   … to …   =B11&" "&B12&" "&B13

What we are doing in the second version is concatenating spaces in between each input cell. Thus, B11 is the first thing we are concatenating, a space (represented by " " in the formula) is the second thing we are concatenating, B12 is the third thing we are concatenating, another space is the

---

[9] In this context, concatenate simply means "to join together."

fourth thing we are concatenating and the fifth and last thing we are concatenating in this example is B13.

There are other formulas, but these are the basics you need for an *Excel Breakthrough*. When you learn these in this book, you will get a feel for how they work and have a methodology. You will then have an instinctual feel for how all the Text formulas in Excel work and how to use them in conjunction to produce powerful results.

Relative and Absolute Cell References

(This lesson uses the file `Cell References.xls` available at www.excelbreakthrough.com.)

Relative Cell References

Suppose we have the simple table shown at right where we are trying to determine the tax on various Subtotals where Tax was simply the Subtotal multiplied by the Tax Rate.

	A	B
1	Tax Rate	8%
2		
3	Subtotal:	Tax:
4	$10.00	$0.80
5	$15.00	
6	$20.00	
7	$25.00	
8	$30.00	

B4   ▼   *fx* =A4*B1

	A	B	C	D
1	Tax Rate	8%		
2				
3	Subtotal:	Tax:		
4	$10.00	$0.80		
5	$15.00			
6	$20.00			
7	$25.00			
8	$30.00			

So in cell B4 we simply put the formula =A4*B1 as shown at left.

Using Control Method, we highlight B4:B8 as shown:

	A	B	C
1	Tax Rate	8%	
2			
3	Subtotal:	Tax:	
4	$10.00	$0.80	
5	$15.00		
6	$20.00		
7	$25.00		
8	$30.00		
9			

Then we hit Ctrl+D to fill in the formulas:

B8		▼		fx	=A8*B5	
	A	B	C	D		
1	Tax Rate	8%				
2						
3	Subtotal:	Tax:				
4	$10.00	$0.80				
5	$15.00	$0.00				
6	$20.00	#VALUE!				
7	$25.00	$20.00				
8	$30.00	$0.00				
9						

Obviously this did not do what we wanted. In the image above we can see the formula in cell B8 as =A8*B5. We know it should be =A8*B1. But when we do a Fill down (or Fill right) in Excel, or when we copy formulas from one range to another, by default Excel will update the formula cell references.

Examining the formulas in the image above closer, we would find:

Cell:	Current formula:	What the formula should be:
B5	=A5*B2	=A5*B1
B6	=A6*B3	=A6*B1
B7	=A7*B3	=A7*B1
B8	=A8*B4	=A8*B1

So if we set up a table as above and realize we needed to fix the formulas manually, doing it four times is not a problem. But imagine if we had 4,000 formulas to fix. We definitely would *not* want to do that manually. This is where absolute cell references save us time—lots of time.

Absolute Cell References

Now consider the situation when we put the formula =A4*$B$1 into cell B4 first:

B4		▼		fx	=A4*$B$1	
	A	B	C	D		
1	Tax Rate	8%				
2						
3	Subtotal:	Tax:				
4	$10.00	$0.80				
5	$15.00					
6	$20.00					
7	$25.00					
8	$30.00					
9						

After we do the same Fill down we get:

	B8	▼	f_x =A8*$B$1	
	A	B	C	D
1	Tax Rate	8%		
2				
3	Subtotal:	Tax:		
4	$10.00	$0.80		
5	$15.00	$1.20		
6	$20.00	$1.60		
7	$25.00	$2.00		
8	$30.00	$2.40		
9				

Now when we did the Fill down the reference to cell B1 stayed *absolute*. We did this by adding the dollar signs ($) before the column and row references in the formula.

Reference pattern:	What it does:
$B$1	Keeps the row and column references absolute.
B$1	Keeps the row reference absolute and the column reference relative.
$B1	Keeps the column reference absolute and the row reference relative.
B1	Keeps the row and column references relative.

The F4 Key (for use with Formulas)

The way to quickly add absolute cell references in formulas is to hit the F4 key when making a formula. Going back to our example, consider the moment in which we are creating the first formula in B4. Let's break down exactly what we would do in detail:

1. Select B4.
2. Hit =.

	SUMIF	▼ X ✓ f_x =	
	A	B	C
1	Tax Rate	8%	
2			
3	Subtotal:	Tax:	
4	$10.00	=	

3. Select A4.

	SUMIF	▼ X ✓ f_x =A4	
	A	B	C
1	Tax Rate	8%	
2			
3	Subtotal:	Tax:	
4	$10.00	=A4	

4. Hit * and then select B1 to get:

SUMIF		▼ ✗ ✓ *fx* =A4*B1		
	A	B	C	D
1	Tax Rate	8%		
2				
3	Subtotal:	Tax:		
4	$10.00	=A4*B1		
5	$15.00			

5. It's at <u>this</u> point after step 4 that we can hit the F4 key. Hitting F4 once yields:

SUMIF		▼ ✗ ✓ *fx* =A4*$B$1		
	A	B	C	D
1	Tax Rate	8%		
2				
3	Subtotal:	Tax:		
4	$10.00	=A4*$B$1		
5	$15.00			

6. As you can see above, F4 automatically added the dollar signs. If we hit it again it will cycle to B$1. Hitting it a third time will cycle it to $B1. Hitting a fourth time will loop it back to B1 (having no absolute references). You can keep hitting F4 to continue cycling through the four options.

Hitting F4 while editing a formula cycles the status of the absolute/relative references on the cell or range in that part of the formula.

Nested Formulas

The next method to master to have an *Excel Breakthrough* is nested formulas. Here's how we define a nested formula:

Nested Formula = a formula inside another formula!

It's that simple. Nested formulas can often help you avoid writing Visual Basic code to do many data processing tasks. We saw an example of this above with a nested IF formula. We'll see examples of this in Part 3 coming up next.

Part 3
Real World Problems

Here we are at the end. By now you have experienced the essential material needed to have a breakthrough in using Excel. The only thing left to do is take on more complex scenarios that really dig into and integrate the most important concepts. And like an architect, you don't need to see the blueprints of every building ever made to learn design. What you need is experiential learning where you stretch yourself.

The scenarios in Part 3 include:

- Extracting Text
- Duplicate Rows
- Average Media Campaign Length
- Transposing Data
- Transposing Data with a Translation Table
- Alternating Row Formats
- Managing Yourself

Problem 1 – Extracting Text

(This problem uses the file `Extract Text.xls` available at www.excelbreakthrough.com.)

	A	B	C
1	SKU 96305263		
2	SKU 35121703		
3	SKU 51377087		
4	SKU 95507267		
5	SKU 97998197		
6	SKU 61425550		
7	SKU 81455192		
8	SKU 92572855		
9	SKU 79143567		
10	SKU 90106965		
11	SKU 61637204		
12	SKU 60111769		
13	SKU 78811152		
14	SKU 25457259		
15	SKU 36872272		
16	SKU 43713232		
17	SKU 28787190		
18	SKU 40121966		
19	SKU 58961596		
20	SKU 82965608		

One of the most common problems clients come to me with is extracting text from cells in long lists. When you have only a few rows on a list, it's no big deal. But what if you have 50 or 100 rows? What about 5,000 rows? Consider the following examples:

Example 1: Regular Text Length

(This example uses the tab "Example 1" in the file `Extract Text.xls` available at www.excelbreakthrough.com.)

Suppose you have a list of Product SKUs all the same length, such as "SKU 12345678" as shown at right.

And pretend this list is 5,000 rows long, though the image here only shows the first 20 rows. Suppose you needed the SKU numbers without the "SKU" attached to it. The fastest and easiest way to do that is as follows:

1. Select A1.
2. Ctrl+Shift+Down to highlight A1:A5000.
3. Alt–D–E to open Convert Text to Columns Wizard.

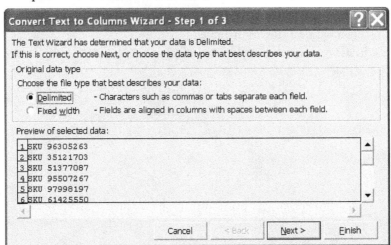

4. Select Fixed width, then click Next. Notice that you could hit Down once to select Fixed width and then hit Enter to go to Step 2 in the wizard.

5.   Next the wizard gives you a preview of where the text will be split:

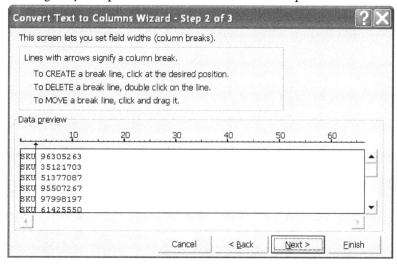

6.   Hit Enter to go to Step 3:

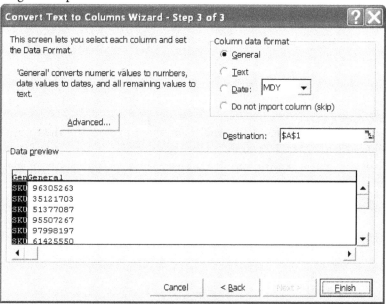

Usually in step 3 we don't need to make any changes to what the wizard will do to the data unless we specifically want to format new columns in particular ways, such as a date format. In this case we won't tweak any options.

7.   Hit Enter to finish the wizard. The result is shown at right.

Very simple, right? The more you use the Convert Text to Columns Wizard the faster you will be with it and very quickly you'll be saying to yourself "Alt–D–E" when you want to split columns this way.

	A	B
1	SKU	96305263
2	SKU	35121703
3	SKU	51377087
4	SKU	95507267
5	SKU	97998197
6	SKU	61425550
7	SKU	81455192
8	SKU	92572855
9	SKU	79143567
10	SKU	90106965

Example 2: Regular Text Length

(This example uses the tab "Example 2" in the file `Extract Text.xls` available at www.excelbreakthrough.com.)

Now suppose we have another table with rows that look like those shown at right.

Again, assume we want to quickly extract the SKUs at the right of each cell.

1. Select A1.

2. Ctrl+Shift+Down to highlight A1:A5000.

3. Alt-D-E to open the Convert Text to Columns Wizard.

	A
1	PR 247625 SKU 71336778
2	PR 287605438 SKU 86905806
3	PR 14343036 SKU 23048698
4	PR 88410 SKU 82395171
5	PR 37046382950 SKU 24104027
6	PR 11620444 SKU 46778294
7	PR 2233904 SKU 30761404
8	PR 11856407 SKU 28882079
9	PR 264251423063 SKU 72026578
10	PR 175520492 SKU 94156236
11	PR 206944 SKU 29530333
12	PR 4700162998318 SKU 38534847
13	PR 18231596 SKU 71861268
14	PR 18403396 SKU 70645023
15	PR 244932 SKU 25907291
16	PR 294682 SKU 56635972
17	PR 40194476 SKU 43017933
18	PR 47806488 SKU 254447
19	PR 87251 SKU 20058790
20	PR 11021173 SKU 18505299

4. For right now, at Step 1 select Fixed width and move to Step 2 in the wizard. The dialog below shows what we see. Notice that if we try to create any break lines to isolate the SKU numbers at the right we can't do it. Instead we have to go back to Step 1 and select Delimited.

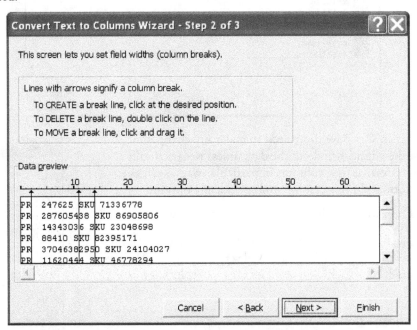

5. So we select Delimited in Step 1 and go to Step 2, as shown below. Notice by default that the wizard selects Tab as the Delimiter. But you can see in the data preview above that it doesn't do anything.

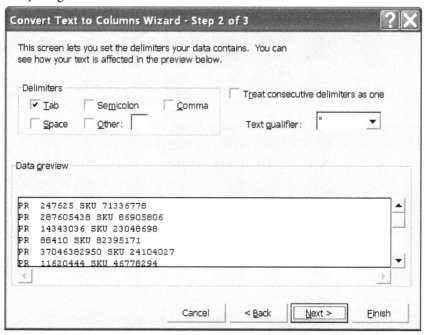

6. Still in Step 2, select Space from the Delimiters list:

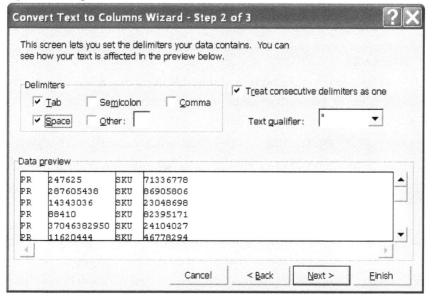

Now notice in the Data preview that the columns will be split accordingly. Also notice to the right of the Delimiters select box there is a checkbox for "Treat consecutive delimiters as one" got checked automatically by the wizard when we selected the Space delimiter. This is used in case there are multiple spaces between text characters in the cells.

7. However, we don't need that extra blank column between PR and the first set of numbers so we'll leave the consecutive delimiters option checked and go to Step 3 and then finish:

	A	B	C	D
1	PR	247625	SKU	71336778
2	PR	2.88E+08	SKU	86905806
3	PR	14343036	SKU	23048698
4	PR	88410	SKU	82395171
5	PR	3.7E+10	SKU	24104027

Example 3: Irregular Text Length at End of Field

(This example uses the tab "Example 3" in the file `Extract Text.xls` available at www.excelbreakthrough.com.)

Now suppose the text is strung together with no spaces. How could we extract the SKU? If we look at our data set shown at right we see that SKUs seem to be 8 digits long.

	A
1	PR247625SKU71336778
2	PR287605438SKU86905806
3	PR14343036SKU23048698
4	PR88410SKU82395171
5	PR37046382950SKU24104027
6	PR47806488SKU254447

The quick solution is as follows:

1. Select B1.
2. Enter formula =RIGHT(A1,8)

B1	fx =RIGHT(A1,8)	
	A	B
1	PR247625SKU71336778	71336778
2	PR287605438SKU86905806	

3. With the formula entered, we need to Fill down to the bottom of the table.
   a. Select A1.
   b. Ctrl+Down to get to the bottom of the table in column A.
   c. Right to get to column B at the bottom of the table.
   d. Ctrl+Shift+Up to highlight up to B1.
   e. Ctrl+D to Fill down.

4. Here is what the result looks like that shown at right (the top of the list, anyway).

B1	fx =RIGHT(A1,8)	
	A	B
1	PR247625SKU71336778	71336778
2	PR287605438SKU86905806	86905806
3	PR14343036SKU23048698	23048698
4	PR88410SKU82395171	82395171
5	PR37046382950SKU24104027	24104027
6	PR47806488SKU254447	KU254447

5. Now we can copy and paste the values in column B in place or somewhere else where we need just the list of SKU numbers. But if you look closely something is off...

6. Look at row **6** in the image above. The SKU is only 6 characters long, not 8. In row **6** the extracted SKU has the letters "KU" at the start of it. Thus, this method didn't exactly work. If all SKUs are exactly 8 characters this would have been fine, but now we need to try something else.

Example 4: Irregular Text Length in Middle of Field

(This example uses the tab "Example 4" in the file `Extract Text.xls` available at www.excelbreakthrough.com.)

	A
1	PR247625SKU71336778
2	PR287605438SKU86905806
3	PR14343036SKU23048698
4	PR88410SKU82395171
5	PR37046382950SKU24104027
6	PR47806488SKU254447

In Example 3 above we assumed the SKU length after the letters "SKU" were all the same. But since they weren't, the above formula didn't do the trick. In other words, the number of digits in the text string before the letters SKU is not always the same and the number of digits in the SKU numbers is not always the same. We are going to need a more complex formula to extract the SKU numbers.

I'm going to show you one formulaic method that may not be the most efficient, but it will get your brain thinking in the *Excel Breakthrough* way. These will be nested formulas, so I'm going to break them up into different cells before merging them into one long nested formula so you can break it down.

Here's a formulaic way to extract only the SKU numbers, i.e., only the digits to the right of the letters "SKU" in each cell:

1. In **B1** enter formula =LEN(A1) as shown:

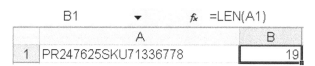

This yields the total length of the text string in **A1**.

2. In **C1** enter the formula =FIND("U",A1,1) as shown:

This yields the starting place of the text "U" in the string in **A1**. Because "U" only occurs once in the string, we can have the FIND formula search for it. If there was another "U" at the beginning we would have to get more specific about what to look for by either setting the starting point of FIND further down the string or search for "SKU."

Note: FIND is case sensitive so if you had a "u" and "U" in the string, the formula would distinguish between them.

3. In D1 enter formula =RIGHT(A1,B1-C1) as shown and fill the formula down to the bottom of the table:

D1		▼	f_x =RIGHT(A1,B1-C1)	

	A	B	C	D
1	PR247625SKU71336778	19	11	71336778
2	PR287605438SKU86905806	22	14	86905806
3	PR14343036SKU23048698	21	13	23048698
4	PR88410SKU82395171	18	10	82395171
5	PR37046382950SKU24104027	24	16	24104027
6	PR47806488SKU254447	19	13	254447

Column D shows the exact SKU number, regardless of length. In other words, this extracts all the digits to the right of the "U" in the text in column A.

While the above solution works, we could have used a nested formula instead that would consolidate all the formulas in columns B, C and D. That nested formula in B1 would be as follows:

=RIGHT(A1,LEN(A1)–FIND("U",A1,1))

Problem 2 – Duplicate Rows

(This problem uses the file `Duplicate Rows.xls` available at www.excelbreakthrough.com.)

One of my clients called me in a panic once because he had a list in Excel over 2,500 lines long. There were three columns of data, which here we'll call our ever trusty Market, Customer and Product. There were many duplicate rows and he needed to get rid of them before sending the list to someone else in his department. His method of finding duplicates was to sort the list and then manually scan for duplicates and simply delete them. In a much shorter list this method would be fine, but with over 2,500 rows this method would have caused him to pull his hair out.

Using our disguised *Excel Breakthrough* data, here is how that list was structured:

	A	B	C
1	Market	Customer	Product
2	SoCal	Ace Computer	Security Suite
3	St. Louis	Elite Software Sales	Disk Suite
4	NorCal	Elite Software Sales	Audit Pro
5	Florida	Ace Computer	Benchmark Tools Basic
6	St. Louis	Powertech	Virus Begone
7	Chicago Region	Media Edge Interactive	Security Suite
8	St. Louis	Ace Computer	Code Cruncher
9	NorCal	Computronics	Office Tools Elite
10	NorCal	Elite Software Sales	Audit Pro
11	St. Louis	Powertech	Disk Suite
12	Mountain South	Bigtech Commerce	Audit Standard
13	St. Louis	Sygell Distributors	Browser Central
14	Pittsburg	Computronics	Virus Begone
15	PacNW	Media Edge Interactive	Web Speed Ultra
16	NYC	Falcon Retail	Security Suite
17	St. Louis	Computronics	Web Speed Ultra
18	St. Louis	Powertech	Code Cruncher
19	NorCal	Bigtech Commerce	Office Tools Plus
20	NorCal	Ace Computer	Office Tools Plus
21	NorCal	Computronics	Office Tools Elite
22	Carolinas	Ace Computer	Code Cruncher
23	PacNW	R-Tek Tronics	Office Tools Professional
24	Chicago Region	Elite Software Sales	Spelling Challenge

To get rid of the duplicates, here is what we did:

1. Sort the list by Market, then by Customer and then by Product.
   a. Right away we can see there are *many* duplicates and to manually delete them as my client proposed would have taken a long time:

	A	B	C
1	Market	Customer	Product
2	Atlanta	Ace Computer	Audit Pro
3	Atlanta	Ace Computer	Audit Pro
4	Atlanta	Ace Computer	Audit Pro
5	Atlanta	Ace Computer	Audit Pro
6	Atlanta	Ace Computer	Audit Pro
7	Atlanta	Ace Computer	Audit Pro
8	Atlanta	Ace Computer	Audit Pro
9	Atlanta	Ace Computer	Audit Pro
10	Atlanta	Ace Computer	Audit Pro
11	Atlanta	Ace Computer	Benchmark Tools Pro
12	Atlanta	Ace Computer	Benchmark Tools Pro
13	Atlanta	Ace Computer	Benchmark Tools Pro
14	Atlanta	Ace Computer	Benchmark Tools Pro
15	Atlanta	Ace Computer	Benchmark Tools Pro
16	Atlanta	Ace Computer	Benchmark Tools Pro
17	Atlanta	Ace Computer	Benchmark Tools Pro
18	Atlanta	Ace Computer	Benchmark Tools Pro
19	Atlanta	Ace Computer	Benchmark Tools Pro
20	Atlanta	Ace Computer	Benchmark Tools Pro
21	Atlanta	Ace Computer	Benchmark Tools Pro
22	Atlanta	Ace Computer	Web Speed Ultra
23	Atlanta	Ace Computer	Web Speed Ultra
24	Atlanta	Ace Computer	Web Speed Ultra

2. In D2 enter the formula =CONCATENATE(A2,B2,C2) as shown below:

D2		▼	*fx* =CONCATENATE(A2,B2,C2)	
	A	B	C	D
1	Market	Customer	Product	
2	Atlanta	Ace Computer	Audit Pro	AtlantaAce ComputerAudit Pro

3. Fill the formula in D2 down to the end of the list using Control Method:
   a. Select C2.
   b. Ctrl+Down to get to bottom of the list in column C.
   c. Right once to move over to column D.
   d. Ctrl+Shift+Up to highlight column D from the bottom of the table to the top.
   e. Ctrl+D to Fill down.

4. Now lets look at the top of the list:

	A	B	C	D
1	**Market**	**Customer**	**Product**	
2	Atlanta	Ace Computer	Audit Pro	AtlantaAce ComputerAudit Pro
3	Atlanta	Ace Computer	Audit Pro	AtlantaAce ComputerAudit Pro
4	Atlanta	Ace Computer	Audit Pro	AtlantaAce ComputerAudit Pro
5	Atlanta	Ace Computer	Audit Pro	AtlantaAce ComputerAudit Pro
6	Atlanta	Ace Computer	Audit Pro	AtlantaAce ComputerAudit Pro
7	Atlanta	Ace Computer	Audit Pro	AtlantaAce ComputerAudit Pro
8	Atlanta	Ace Computer	Audit Pro	AtlantaAce ComputerAudit Pro
9	Atlanta	Ace Computer	Audit Pro	AtlantaAce ComputerAudit Pro
10	Atlanta	Ace Computer	Audit Pro	AtlantaAce ComputerAudit Pro
11	Atlanta	Ace Computer	Benchmark Tools Pro	AtlantaAce ComputerBenchmark Tools Pro
12	Atlanta	Ace Computer	Benchmark Tools Pro	AtlantaAce ComputerBenchmark Tools Pro
13	Atlanta	Ace Computer	Benchmark Tools Pro	AtlantaAce ComputerBenchmark Tools Pro
14	Atlanta	Ace Computer	Benchmark Tools Pro	AtlantaAce ComputerBenchmark Tools Pro
15	Atlanta	Ace Computer	Benchmark Tools Pro	AtlantaAce ComputerBenchmark Tools Pro
16	Atlanta	Ace Computer	Benchmark Tools Pro	AtlantaAce ComputerBenchmark Tools Pro
17	Atlanta	Ace Computer	Benchmark Tools Pro	AtlantaAce ComputerBenchmark Tools Pro
18	Atlanta	Ace Computer	Benchmark Tools Pro	AtlantaAce ComputerBenchmark Tools Pro
19	Atlanta	Ace Computer	Benchmark Tools Pro	AtlantaAce ComputerBenchmark Tools Pro
20	Atlanta	Ace Computer	Benchmark Tools Pro	AtlantaAce ComputerBenchmark Tools Pro
21	Atlanta	Ace Computer	Benchmark Tools Pro	AtlantaAce ComputerBenchmark Tools Pro
22	Atlanta	Ace Computer	Web Speed Ultra	AtlantaAce ComputerWeb Speed Ultra
23	Atlanta	Ace Computer	Web Speed Ultra	AtlantaAce ComputerWeb Speed Ultra

5. In E2 enter the formula =IF(EXACT(D2,D1),1,0) as shown below:

fx =IF(EXACT(D2,D1),1,0)

B	C	D	E
tomer	**Product**		
Computer	Audit Pro	AtlantaAce ComputerAudit Pro	0

  a. This means, "If the value in D2 is the same as the value in D1, put 1 in E2, otherwise put 0 in E2."
  b. Fill the formula in E2 down to the bottom of the list using Control Method.

6. Copy and paste the values of columns D:E in place:
  a. While still in column E, hit Ctrl+Spacebar.
  b. Shift+Left to highlight columns D:E.
  c. Ctrl+C to copy.
  d. Alt–E–S–V–Enter to paste values in place. We want to have values in this column and not *formulas* because we are going to search for the first occurrence of 1 once we sort the list.

Here is our list at this point:

	A	B	C	D	E
1	**Market**	**Customer**	**Product**		
2	Atlanta	Ace Computer	Audit Pro	AtlantaAce ComputerAudit Pro	0
3	Atlanta	Ace Computer	Audit Pro	AtlantaAce ComputerAudit Pro	1
4	Atlanta	Ace Computer	Audit Pro	AtlantaAce ComputerAudit Pro	1
5	Atlanta	Ace Computer	Audit Pro	AtlantaAce ComputerAudit Pro	1
6	Atlanta	Ace Computer	Audit Pro	AtlantaAce ComputerAudit Pro	1
7	Atlanta	Ace Computer	Audit Pro	AtlantaAce ComputerAudit Pro	1
8	Atlanta	Ace Computer	Audit Pro	AtlantaAce ComputerAudit Pro	1
9	Atlanta	Ace Computer	Audit Pro	AtlantaAce ComputerAudit Pro	1
10	Atlanta	Ace Computer	Audit Pro	AtlantaAce ComputerAudit Pro	1
11	Atlanta	Ace Computer	Benchmark Tools Pro	AtlantaAce ComputerBenchmark Tools Pro	0
12	Atlanta	Ace Computer	Benchmark Tools Pro	AtlantaAce ComputerBenchmark Tools Pro	1
13	Atlanta	Ace Computer	Benchmark Tools Pro	AtlantaAce ComputerBenchmark Tools Pro	1
14	Atlanta	Ace Computer	Benchmark Tools Pro	AtlantaAce ComputerBenchmark Tools Pro	1
15	Atlanta	Ace Computer	Benchmark Tools Pro	AtlantaAce ComputerBenchmark Tools Pro	1

In column E, any row with the value 0 is a row we want to keep. All the rows with the value 1 in column E are the duplicates.

7. Sort the list on column E ascending.
    a. Make sure you don't sort the column headers.
    b. This will push all the duplicates to the bottom of the list.

	A	B	C	D	E
1	**Market**	**Customer**	**Product**		
2	Atlanta	Ace Computer	Audit Pro	AtlantaAce ComputerAudit Pro	0
3	Atlanta	Ace Computer	Benchmark Tools Pro	AtlantaAce ComputerBenchmark Tools Pro	0
4	Atlanta	Ace Computer	Web Speed Ultra	AtlantaAce ComputerWeb Speed Ultra	0
5	Atlanta	Bigtech Commerce	Code Cruncher	AtlantaBigtech CommerceCode Cruncher	0
6	Atlanta	Media Edge Interactive	Photo Organizer	AtlantaMedia Edge InteractivePhoto Organizer	0
7	Atlanta	Powertech	Code Cruncher	AtlantaPowertechCode Cruncher	0
8	Atlanta	Powertech	Photo Organizer	AtlantaPowertechPhoto Organizer	0
9	Atlanta	Powertech	Presentation Spiffer	AtlantaPowertechPresentation Spiffer	0
10	Atlanta	Powertech	Web Speed Ultra	AtlantaPowertechWeb Speed Ultra	0
11	Atlanta	Sygell Distributors	Web Speed Ultra	AtlantaSygell DistributorsWeb Speed Ultra	0
12	Boston	Ace Computer	Presentation Spiffer	BostonAce ComputerPresentation Spiffer	0
13	Boston	Ace Computer	Security Suite	BostonAce ComputerSecurity Suite	0
14	Boston	Computronics	Office Tools Basic	BostonComputronicsOffice Tools Basic	0
15	Boston	Falcon Retail	Disk Suite	BostonFalcon RetailDisk Suite	0
16	Boston	Falcon Retail	Office Tools Basic	BostonFalcon RetailOffice Tools Basic	0
17	Boston	Media Edge Interactive	Math Wizard	BostonMedia Edge InteractiveMath Wizard	0

8. Highlight only column E.
    a. Select E1. Try using Control Method.
    b. Ctrl+Spacebar.

9. Ctrl+F to open Find and search for the value 1:

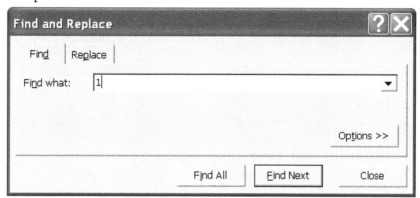

10. This will take you to the start of the duplicate rows:

	A	B	C	D	E
1	Market	Customer	Product		
293	Texas	Computronics	Audit Standard	TexasComputronicsAudit Standard	0
294	Texas	Powertech	Web Speed Ultra	TexasPowertechWeb Speed Ultra	0
295	Washington D.C.	Ace Computer	Office Tools Plus	Washington D.C.Ace ComputerOffice Tools Plus	0
296	Washington D.C.	Elite Software Sales	Browser Central	Washington D.C.Elite Software SalesBrowser Central	0
297	Washington D.C.	Media Edge Interactive	Web Speed Ultra	Washington D.C.Media Edge InteractiveWeb Speed Ultra	0
298	Washington D.C.	Powertech	Benchmark Tools Basic	Washington D.C.PowertechBenchmark Tools Basic	0
299	Washington D.C.	Powertech	Web Speed Ultra	Washington D.C.PowertechWeb Speed Ultra	0
300	Atlanta	Ace Computer	Audit Pro	AtlantaAce ComputerAudit Pro	1
301	Atlanta	Ace Computer	Audit Pro	AtlantaAce ComputerAudit Pro	1

11. Our duplicates start at row 300, so with cell E300 selected (shown above) we do the following to get rid of the duplicates once and for all:
   a. Shift+Spacebar to highlight all of row 300.
   b. Ctrl+Shift+Down to highlight all the duplicate rows (down to row 2685).
   c. Hit the Menu button.
   d. Hit D to delete the duplicate rows!

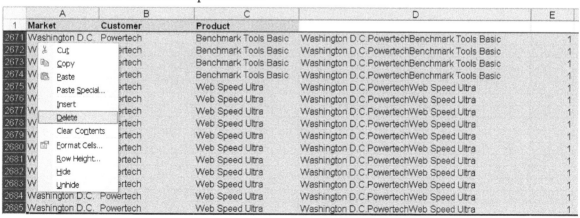

12. Finally, we can delete the temporary data in columns D and E.
   a. Select columns D:E.

b. Delete the content or delete the actual columns. I prefer highlighting the columns
    using Ctrl+Spacebar and Menu–D.

	A	B	C
1	**Market**	**Customer**	**Product**
2	Atlanta	Ace Computer	Audit Pro
3	Atlanta	Ace Computer	Benchmark Tools Pro
4	Atlanta	Ace Computer	Web Speed Ultra
5	Atlanta	Bigtech Commerce	Code Cruncher
6	Atlanta	Media Edge Interactive	Photo Organizer
7	Atlanta	Powertech	Code Cruncher
8	Atlanta	Powertech	Photo Organizer
9	Atlanta	Powertech	Presentation Spiffer
10	Atlanta	Powertech	Web Speed Ultra
11	Atlanta	Sygell Distributors	Web Speed Ultra
12	Boston	Ace Computer	Presentation Spiffer
13	Boston	Ace Computer	Security Suite
14	Boston	Computronics	Office Tools Basic
15	Boston	Falcon Retail	Disk Suite
16	Boston	Falcon Retail	Office Tools Basic
17	Boston	Media Edge Interactive	Math Wizard
18	Boston	Media Edge Interactive	Office Tools Professional
19	Boston	Powertech	Code Cruncher
20	Boston	Powertech	Security Suite

And that's it! This *Excel Breakthrough* method usually takes less than 60 seconds to do, especially
when you maximize the use of keyboard shortcuts.

Problem 3 – Average Media Campaign Length

(This problem uses the file `Media Spending.xls` available at www.excelbreakthrough.com.)

Consider the "Media Spend" table as shown at right.

This table shows the dollar amount of media spending in each time period in each state, where state can be rolled up into various regions. The time periods are months in the years 2004 through 2007 in the Mon-YY date format as shown. The full table has nearly 450 rows.

What if we wanted to know the average media campaign length in each state and region, measured in months?

For example, if we know that the first month of spending in a particular state was Jan-05 and the last month of spending in that state was Nov-06, then regardless of how many months in between there was active spending we could measure the total campaign length as 23 months.

	A	B	C	D
1	Region	State	Time Period	Media Spend
2	Northwest	Washington	Feb-04	$4,344
3	Northwest	Washington	Mar-04	$9,027
4	Northwest	Washington	Apr-04	$2,688
5	Northwest	Washington	May-04	$2,210
6	Northwest	Washington	Jun-04	$855
7	Northwest	Washington	Jul-04	$10,004
8	Mid Atlantic	Pennsylvania	Jul-04	$16,036
9	Northwest	Washington	Aug-04	$13,987
10	Mid Atlantic	Pennsylvania	Aug-04	$106
11	Northwest	Washington	Sep-04	$1,399
12	Mid Atlantic	Pennsylvania	Sep-04	$5,638
13	Northwest	Washington	Oct-04	$757
14	Mid Atlantic	Pennsylvania	Oct-04	$131
15	Northwest	Washington	Nov-04	$193
16	Mid Atlantic	Pennsylvania	Nov-04	$104
17	Northwest	Washington	Dec-04	$7,512
18	Mid Atlantic	Pennsylvania	Dec-04	$596
19	Southeast	Atlanta	Jan-05	$456
20	West	California	Jan-05	$1,937

We could sort the list by state and then by time period as in the image below where we happen to see all the data for the first alphabetic state on our list, Alaska:

The first month of spending in Alaska is Apr-05 and the last month is Apr-07. Notice that in some months there was no activity in Alaska, such as Aug-05. That doesn't matter as all we are interested in is the first and last months of activity to measure the total duration of the campaign. In Alaska's case, this means the campaign was 25 months long.

It is a bit tedious to determine the campaign length for each state (and region) this way. Luckily, there is a much faster way of doing it that involves two bonus formulas, MONTH and YEAR.

- MONTH yields the numeric month based on a date format input
  - MONTH(Jan-05) returns the value 1 because January is the 1st month on the calendar

	A	B	C	D
1	Region	State	Time Period	Media Spend
2	Pacific	Alaska	Apr-05	$9,473
3	Pacific	Alaska	May-05	$9,179
4	Pacific	Alaska	Jun-05	$6,843
5	Pacific	Alaska	Jul-05	$1,010
6	Pacific	Alaska	Oct-05	$567
7	Pacific	Alaska	Nov-05	$360
8	Pacific	Alaska	Dec-05	$939
9	Pacific	Alaska	Jan-06	$133
10	Pacific	Alaska	Feb-06	$1,037
11	Pacific	Alaska	Mar-06	$637
12	Pacific	Alaska	Apr-06	$175
13	Pacific	Alaska	Jul-06	$715
14	Pacific	Alaska	Aug-06	$14,737
15	Pacific	Alaska	Sep-06	$6,417
16	Pacific	Alaska	Oct-06	$12,406
17	Pacific	Alaska	Nov-06	$17,368
18	Pacific	Alaska	Dec-06	$515
19	Pacific	Alaska	Jan-07	$2,087
20	Pacific	Alaska	Feb-07	$13,216
21	Pacific	Alaska	Mar-07	$2,103
22	Pacific	Alaska	Apr-07	$5,382

- ° MONTH(Feb-06) returns the value 2 because February is the 2nd month on the calendar
- ° Etc...
- YEAR yields the four digit year based on a date format input
  - ° YEAR(Jan-05) returns the value 2005
  - ° YEAR(Apr-06) returns the value 2006

These two simple formulas will lead us to our quick solution.

Here's what to do:

1. Enter the text "Year" in E1.

2. Enter the text "Month" in F1.

3. In E2 enter the formula =YEAR(C2) as shown below:

E2		f_x =YEAR(C2)			
	A	B	C	D	E	F
1	Region	State	Time Period	Media Spend	Year	Month
2	Northwest	Washington	Feb-04	$4,344	2004	
3	Northwest	Washington	Mar-04	$9,027		

4. In F2 enter the formula =MONTH(C2) as shown below:

F2		f_x =MONTH(C2)			
	A	B	C	D	E	F
1	Region	State	Time Period	Media Spend	Year	Month
2	Northwest	Washington	Feb-04	$4,344	2004	2
3	Northwest	Washington	Mar-04	$9,027		

5. Enter the text "Total Months" in G1.

6. In G2 enter the formula =E2*12+F2 as shown below:

G2		f_x =E2*12+F2				
	A	B	C	D	E	F	G
1	Region	State	Time Period	Media Spend	Year	Month	Total Months
2	Northwest	Washington	Feb-04	$4,344	2004	2	24050
3	Northwest	Washington	Mar-04	$9,027			

Note that in the formula in G2 we are multiplying the year (E2) by 12, as in the number twelve. Don't misread what's written here as a cell reference to I2. We do this to convert the year into months. In other words, how many months are there in 2,004 years? There are 12 * 2004 which equals 24,048 months. Adding this to the number of the month in F2 yields 24,050 in G2.

7. Now we use Control Method to fill the formulas in E2:G2 down to the bottom of the table:
   a. Select D2.
   b. Ctrl+Down to get to the bottom of the table in column D.
   c. Right to get to column E at the bottom of the table:

	A	B	C	D	E	F	G
1	**Region**	**State**	**Time Period**	**Media Spend**	**Year**	**Month**	**Total Months**
441	Mountain	Utah	Sep-07	$158			
442	Southeast	Atlanta	Oct-07	$4,451			
443	Southeast	Florida	Oct-07	$8,977			
444	Southeast	S. Carolina	Oct-07	$102			
445	Southeast	S. Carolina	Nov-07	$1,672			
446	Southeast	S. Carolina	Dec-07	$2,724			

   d. Shift+Right to highlight E446:F446.
   e. Shift+Right again to highlight E446:G446.
   f. Ctrl+Shift+Up to highlight E2:G446.
   g. Ctrl+D to fill down the formulas.

G446   ▼   *fx* =E446*12+F446

	A	B	C	D	E	F	G
1	**Region**	**State**	**Time Period**	**Media Spend**	**Year**	**Month**	**Total Months**
443	Southeast	Florida	Oct-07	$8,977	2007	10	24094
444	Southeast	S. Carolina	Oct-07	$102	2007	10	24094
445	Southeast	S. Carolina	Nov-07	$1,672	2007	11	24095
446	Southeast	S. Carolina	Dec-07	$2,724	2007	12	24096

8. Next we need to create a very simple PivotTable.
   a. Select any cell in the table.
   b. Alt–D–P to launch the PivotTable wizard.
   c. Make sure to create the PivotTable on a new sheet. Here is what it will look like:

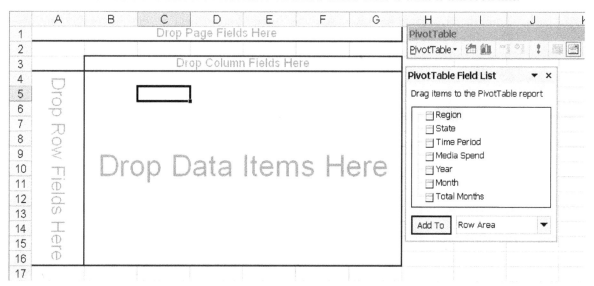

9. Populate the PivotTable as follows:
   a. From the PivotTable Field List, drag the "State" field to where it says "Drop Row Fields Here" in the table, i.e., anywhere in the range A4:A16 shown above. The result will look like the screenshot below:

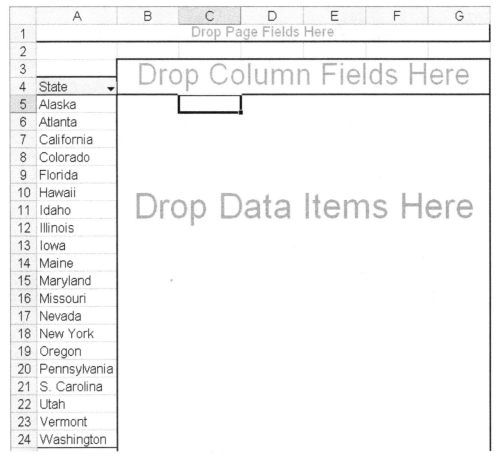

   b. From the PivotTable Field List, drag the "Total Months" field to where it says "Drop Data Items Here" in the table, i.e., anywhere in the range B5:G25 as shown in the image in step 9a above.
   c. Now you are going to repeat step 9b again, so that it looks like you have moved the "Total Months" field into the data range of the PivotTable twice. The result will look like the following:

	A	B	C
1	Drop Page Fields Here		
2			
3	State	Data	Total
4	Alaska	Count of Total Months	21
5		Count of Total Months2	21
6	Atlanta	Count of Total Months	34
7		Count of Total Months2	34
8	California	Count of Total Months	21
9		Count of Total Months2	21

d. Drag the Data header in **B3** to **C3**:

	A	B	C
1		Drop Page Fields Here	
2			
3		Data ▼	
4	State ▼	Count of Total Months	Count of Total Months2
5	Alaska	21	21
6	Atlanta	34	34
7	California	21	21
8	Colorado	27	27
9	Florida	8	8

e. Right click on **B4** (where it says "Count of Total Months").

f. Select Field Settings.

g. Select **Min** and hit OK.

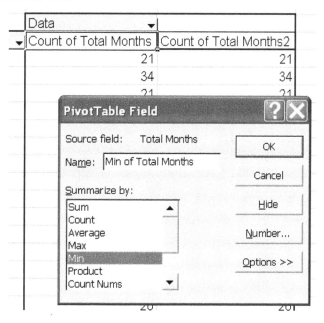

h. Right click on **C4** (where it says "Count of Total Months2").

i. Select Field Settings.

j.   Select **Max** and hit OK. Now our PivotTable looks like the following:

	A	B	C
1		Drop Page Fields Here	
2			
3		Data ▼	
4	State ▼	Min of Total Months	Max of Total Months2
5	Alaska	24064	24088
6	Atlanta	24061	24094
7	California	24061	24083
8	Colorado	24062	24093
9	Florida	24087	24094
10	Hawaii	24070	24083
11	Idaho	24080	24090

10. For each state, if we subtract "Min of TotalMonths" from "Max of TotalMonths2" we will get the campaign length in each state.
   a.   In **D5**, enter the formula **=C5-B5**.
   b.   Fill this formula down to **D24**.
   c.   In **D25**, enter the formula **=AVERAGE(D5:D24)**.

| D25 | ▼ | *fx* =AVERAGE(D5:D24) | | |

	A	B	C	D
1				
2				
3		Data ▼		
4	State ▼	Min of Total Months	Max of Total Months2	
5	Alaska	24064	24088	24
6	Atlanta	24061	24094	33
7	California	24061	24083	22
8	Colorado	24062	24093	31
9	Florida	24087	24094	7
10	Hawaii	24070	24083	13
11	Idaho	24080	24090	10
12	Illinois	24061	24085	24
13	Iowa	24063	24088	25
14	Maine	24076	24084	8
15	Maryland	24065	24080	15
16	Missouri	24063	24093	30
17	Nevada	24068	24086	18
18	New York	24063	24087	24
19	Oregon	24067	24092	25
20	Pennsylvania	24055	24085	30
21	S. Carolina	24061	24096	35
22	Utah	24078	24093	15
23	Vermont	24062	24092	30
24	Washington	24050	24092	42
25	Grand Total	24050	24096	23.05

There we have it! The average campaign length in each state is 23.05 months.

What if we wanted to see the same average but at the regional level?

1. Starting from where we left off, click and drag the State field from A4 in the PivotTable to anywhere outside the PivotTable. The result will look like the following:

	A	B	C	D
1				
2				
3		Data		
4		Min of Total Months	Max of Total Months2	
5	Total	24050	24096	46
6				0
7				0
8				0

2. Drag the Region field to A5, resulting in the following:

	A	B	C	D
1		Drop Page Fields Here		
2				
3		Data		
4	Region	Min of Total Months	Max of Total Months2	
5	Mid Atlantic	24055	24085	30
6	Midwest	24061	24093	32
7	Mountain	24062	24093	31
8	Northeast	24062	24092	30
9	Northwest	24050	24092	42
10	Pacific	24064	24088	24
11	Southeast	24061	24096	35
12	West	24061	24086	25
13	Grand Total	24050	24096	46
14				0
15				0
16				0
17				0
18				0
19				0
20				0
21				0
22				0
23				0
24				0
25				14.75

3. Notice the formulas in column D remained constant. All the formulas in C14:C24 resulting in 0 values are impacting the total average, so simply select C14:C24 and hit Delete to get a quick and dirty answer to the average at the regional level:

	A	B	C	D
1				
2				
3		Data ▼		
4	Region ▼	Min of Total Months	Max of Total Months2	
5	Mid Atlantic	24055	24085	30
6	Midwest	24061	24093	32
7	Mountain	24062	24093	31
8	Northeast	24062	24092	30
9	Northwest	24050	24092	42
10	Pacific	24064	24088	24
11	Southeast	24061	24096	35
12	West	24061	24086	25
13	Grand Total	24050	24096	46
14				
15				
16				
17				
18				
19				
20				
21				
22				
23				
24				
25				32.77778

As shown in the image above, the average campaign length at the regional level is 32.77 months!

Problem 4 – Transposing Data

(This problem uses the file `Transpose Example 1.xls` available at www.excelbreakthrough.com.)

This problem is going to have a long setup section because it is very valuable to understand the fundamental nature of the challenge. Some of my tutoring clients consider this problem one of the worst kinds of challenges they ever had to face and call this the "killer problem to end all Excel problems." I assure you I've had clients with Excel tasks much worse than what you are about to read, but for many Excel users this is about as complex as they would ever consider tackling. This problem will help you appreciate the value of having organization and consistency between different but related tables. Keep that in the back of you mind as you read. Also, the next problem builds on this one.

As a reminder, notice that I give detailed instructions about which keyboard shortcuts to use to reinforce your facility with them. You will find that you are breezing through those instructions with enough practice.

Finally, this problem is a scaled down version of an actual scenario one of my clients came to me with. His two data tables were roughly 10,000 and 500 rows long. In our fictitious data we scale them down to roughly 400 and 50 rows, respectively.

Problem Setup

Imagine we have a Media Spending table on one sheet with over 400 rows containing advertising media spending against various industry products broken down by time period and media type. The top of our Media Spending table look like the following:

	A	B	C	D	E	F	G	H	I	J
1	Media Brand	Time Period	TOTAL	Network TV	Spot TV	Cable TV	Syndicated TV	Print	Trade Print	US Internet
2	BIG FOUR CORP ADT STE PRO SW	Jan-05	162.5						162.5	
3	BIG FOUR CORP ADT STE PRO SW	Feb-05	118						118	
4	BIG FOUR CORP ADT STE PRO SW	Mar-05	122.2					122.2		
5	BIG FOUR CORP ADT STE PRO SW	Apr-05	11.2						11.2	
6	BIG FOUR CORP ADT STE PRO SW	May-05	38.7						38.7	
7	BIG FOUR CORP ADT STE PRO SW	Jun-05	37.8						37.8	
8	BIG FOUR CORP ADT STE PRO SW	Jul-05	54.1						54.1	
9	BIG FOUR CORP ADT STE PRO SW	Aug-05	131.7						131.7	
10	BIG FOUR CORP ADT STE PRO SW	Sep-05	1153.6	235.8	3.2	780.8			125.3	8.5
11	BIG FOUR CORP ADT STE PRO SW	Oct-05	342.3		3.4	175			152.5	11.4
12	BIG FOUR CORP ADT STE PRO SW	Nov-05	1895.6	1347.2	135.3	103.7	185.8		120.6	3
13	BIG FOUR CORP ADT STE PRO SW	Dec-05	24.4		1	23.4				
14	BIG FOUR CORP ADT STE PRO SW	Jan-06	383.9					341.6	42.3	
15	BIG FOUR CORP ADT STE PRO SW	Feb-06	2403	790.1	0	1088.2	11	391.7		122
16	BIG FOUR CORP ADT STE PRO SW	Mar-06	796.4	99.4	0.6	645.1			50.8	0.5
17	BIG FOUR CORP ADT STE PRO SW	Apr-06	16.7		1.3		15.4			
18	BIG FOUR CORP ADT STE PRO SW	May-06	1.2		1.2					
19	BIG FOUR CORP ADT STE PRO SW	Jun-06	3049.6	312.9		2564.3			162.8	9.6
20	BIG FOUR CORP ADT STE PRO SW	Jul-06	826.4			116.1		413	297.3	
21	BIG FOUR CORP ADT STE PRO SW	Aug-06	134.5						134.5	
22	BIG FOUR CORP ADT STE PRO SW	Sep-06	1670.9	330		1015.6			277.2	48.1
23	BIG FOUR CORP ADT STE PRO SW	Oct-06	1057.0			570		122	318.4	28.4

The time periods are simply months, such as Jan-05 as shown above. The media types are listed in the headers along the top in D1:J1. Right away we can see that Media Brands had active spending against them in many time periods against many media types. And remember, this is only the top rows of the table showing data for mostly one Media Brand, "BIG FOUR CORP ADT STE PRO SW." We have no idea what that means yet, but we'll get to that. The table contains 23 unique Media Brands as shown on the list shown at right.

Media Brands
MICROSELLER ASSPY DEF SW
BIG FOUR CORP AUDIT SUITE DLX SW
BIG FOUR CORP ADT STE PRO SW
BIG FOUR CORP STNDRD AUDIT
TECHWERKZ SOFTWARE BENCHMARK BASIC
TECHWERKZ SOFTWARE BENCHMARK PRO
OMNIWEB BROWSER SW
HACKERASSIST CORP CODE CRUNCH SW
TECHWERKZ SOFTWARE DISK SUITE SW
LEARN-TECH INC MATH WIZ
MICROSELLER OFFICE SUITE BASIC SW
MICROSELLER ELITE TOOLS OFFICE SW
MICROSELLER OFFICE PLS TLS SW
MICROSELLER OFFICE PRO TLS SW
OMNIWEB PHOTO DLX SW
OMNIWEB PHOTO BASIC SW
MICROSELLER PRES SPIF TOOLS
BIG FOUR CORP BUNDLE PROD
LOCKNROCK SECURITY SUITE SW
MICROSELLER GRID TOOLS
LEARN-TECH INC SPEL CHLLENGE
LOCKNROCK VIRUS BEG SW
HACKERASSIST CORP WEB ULTRA SPEED

We also have another table of Product Sales shown below:

	A	B	C	D	E	F	G	H	I	J	K	L
1	Product	Total Revenues	Units Sold	Average Sales Price	TOTAL	Network TV	Spot TV	Cable TV	Syndicat ed TV	Print	Trade Print	US Internet
2	Ad-Spy Defense	$35,565,177	1,425,312	$24.95								
3	Audit Deluxe	$46,529,526	1,346,103	$34.57								
4	Audit Pro	$11,589,570	427,025	$27.14								
5	Audit Standard	$25,463,971	957,442	$26.60								
6	Benchmark Tools Basic	$6,519,511	262,932	$24.80								
7	Benchmark Tools Pro	$59,717,367	2,006,864	$29.76								
8	Browser Central	$35,763,262	1,297,332	$27.57								
9	Code Cruncher	$96,826,047	3,148,233	$30.76								
10	Disk Suite	$68,081,550	2,327,837	$29.25								
11	Math Wizard	$28,309,295	1,099,680	$25.74								
12	Office Tools Basic	$36,693,637	1,262,133	$29.07								
13	Office Tools Elite	$173,035,728	5,316,047	$32.55								
14	Office Tools Plus	$54,374,968	1,950,361	$27.88								
15	Office Tools Professional	$54,115,842	1,829,302	$29.58								
16	Photo Deluxe	$16,211,374	697,065	$23.26								
17	Photo Organizer	$131,265,006	4,236,162	$30.99								
18	Presentation Spiffer	$37,183,538	1,342,692	$27.69								
19	Productivity Bundle	$43,274,660	1,426,267	$30.34								
20	Security Suite	$44,687,990	1,564,576	$28.56								
21	Speadsheet Tools	$19,933,796	767,313	$25.98								
22	Spelling Challenge	$20,283,994	741,218	$27.37								
23	Virus Begone	$133,225,801	4,071,017	$32.73								
24	Web Speed Ultra	$132,072,135	4,629,602	$28.53								

If you read into the Media Brands in the first sheet, you'll see that they resemble our product names in the list above from our Product Sales table. Also notice in the Product Sales table above that the empty columns in E:L correspond *exactly* to the media types in the Media Spending table.

So What Are We Trying to Do?

Our task is to get the total of the media spending for each unique Media Brand into the Product Sales sheet. In other words, we need to sum each media type for each Media Brand across all the months and put it into the Product Sales sheet. Confusing? Don't worry, we'll step through it.

Oh, and there's a catch that you have probably noticed already. In the real world with my actual client, we had the dubious problem that Product Sales came from a database provided by one agency and Media Spending came from a different database provided by another agency. These two agencies did not use the same names to match up media with products.

For example: on the Product Sales sheet we see a product called "Audit Deluxe" that was manufactured by Big Four Corp. On the Media Spending sheet we find media spending against this product listed under "BIG FOUR CORP AUDIT SUITE DLX SW." So if you are going to transpose data from Media Spending to Product Sales, you would have to know these translations in your head or have them listed somewhere or else you would be totally lost.

Anyway, for this situation let's just assume that we *do* know all those translations. The following is a relatively easy solution assuming you did not have a huge amount data to transpose:

The Solution
Our solution will use Filtering and the SUBTOTAL Formula.

1. Select the Media Spending sheet and make sure it is sorted by Media Brand and then by Time Period.

2. Add a Freeze Pane between rows 1 and 2 to keep the column headers at the top.
    a. Select A2.
    b. Alt–W–F to insert the Freeze Pane.

3. Insert a row at the top of the table.
    a. Select A1.
    b. Shift+Spacebar to highlight row 1.
    c. Menu-I to insert an empty row.

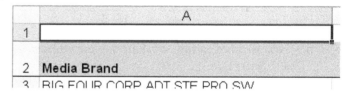

4. Insert Subtotal formulas above the table.
    a. Select C1.
    b. In the cell type =SUBTOTAL(9, as shown:

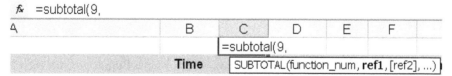

    c. At this point use Down to select C3 as shown:

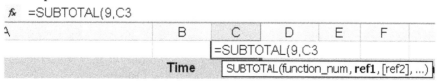

d. Ctrl+Shift+Down to select C3:C435 as shown:

fx =SUBTOTAL(9,C3:C435

\	B	C	D	E	F	G
		=SUBTOTAL(9,C3:C435				
		SUBTOTAL(function_num, **ref1**, [ref2], ...)				di
	Time					
	Period	TOTAL	TV	TV	TV	T
?E DISK SUITE SW	Jun-06	**955.9**			82.8	
?E DISK SUITE SW	Jul-06	**1041.9**		0.4		
?E DISK SUITE SW	Aug-06	**0.4**		0.4		
?E DISK SUITE SW	Sep-06	**1135.6**	586.2		435.6	
?E DISK SUITE SW	Oct-06	**785.8**			435.8	
?E DISK SUITE SW	Nov-06	**0**				
?E DISK SUITE SW	Dec-06	**441.8**			172.1	
?E DISK SUITE SW	Jan-07	**100.9**				

e. Finish the formula with a closed parentheses and hit Enter.

f. Highlight C1:J1.

g. Ctrl+R to Fill right.

fx =SUBTOTAL(9,C3:C435)

A	B	C	D	E	F	G	H	I	J
		246892	58937.5	1915	127733	996.6	18385	23287	15638.5
	Time		Network	Spot	Cable	Syndicated		Trade	US
	Period	TOTAL	TV	TV	TV	TV	Print	Print	Internet
?TE PRO SW	Jan-05	162.5						162.5	

5. Next we need to add AutoFilters to the table.
    a. Select C2.
    b. Alt–D–F–Enter.

	A	B	C	D	E	F	G	H	I	J
1			246892	58937.5	1915	127733	996.6	18385	23287	15638.5
		Time		Network	Spot	Cable	Syndicated		Trade	US
2	Media Brand	Perio ▼	TOT/ ▼	TV ▼	T\ ▼	TV ▼	TV ▼	Prin ▼	Pri ▼	Intern ▼
3	BIG FOUR CORP ADT STE PRO SW	Jan-05	162.5						162.5	
4	BIG FOUR CORP ADT STE PRO SW	Feb-05	118						118	
5	BIG FOUR CORP ADT STE PRO SW	Mar-05	122.2					122.2		
6	BIG FOUR CORP ADT STE PRO SW	Apr-05	11.2						11.2	

6. Now comes the "fun" part, assuming we know which Media Brands go with each Product.
    a. Highlight C1:J1.
    b. Use the Filter in A2 to manually select each Media Brand one at a time. Notice the subtotals in C1:J1 change each time you select a different Media Brand with the Filter in A2.

7. Manually populate the subtotals from the Media Spend sheet to the Product Sales sheet. For the first Product on the Product Sales sheet, Ad-Spy Defense, the Media Brand is MICROSELLER ADSPY DEF SW.
    a. Select MICROSELLER ADSPY DEF SW from the Filter in A2.

b. Since we have C1:J1 highlighted, hit Ctrl+C to copy:

	A	B	C	D	E	F	G	H	I	J
1			5050	2639.8	212.7	693.7	40.2	851.7	506.9	105
			TOTAL	Network	Spot TV	Cable	Syndicated	Print	Trade	US Internet
2	Media Brand	Time Peri	(000)	TV (00	(000)	TV (00	TV (000)	(000)	Print (00	(000)
152	MICROSELLER ADSPY DEF SW	Mar-05	622.6					539.7	82.9	
153	MICROSELLER ADSPY DEF SW	Apr-05	34.6						34.6	
154	MICROSELLER ADSPY DEF SW	May-05	0							0

c. Ctrl+PgUp (or PgDn) to select the Product Sales sheet.

d. On the Product Sales sheet, select E2.

e. Alt–E–S–V–Enter to paste values:

	A	B	C	D	E	F	G	H	I	J	K	L
		Total	Units	Average		Network			Syndicat		Trade	US
1	Product	Revenues	Sold	Sales Price	TOTAL	TV	Spot TV	Cable TV	ed TV	Print	Print	Internet
2	Ad-Spy Defense	$35,565,177	1,425,312	$24.95	5050	2639.8	212.7	693.7	40.2	851.7	506.9	105
3	Audit Deluxe	$46,529,526	1,346,103	$34.57								
4	Audit Pro	$11,589,570	427,025	$27.14								
5	Audit Standard	$25,463,971	957,442	$26.60								

f. Now simply repeat steps a. through e. above for each Product/Media Brand. Obviously, you might have to guess which Media Brand goes with the right Product. To help you out, the included file Transpose Example 1.xls has a Translation Table that lists all these connections.

This isn't a terrible process for just 23 products. The next example takes this a step further with a method we could easily use for 2,300 or 23,000 or more products. And in case you are one step ahead, it uses that supplied Translation Table to make manual copy and paste obsolete.

Problem 5 – Transposing Data with a Translation Table

(This problem uses the file `Transpose Example 2.xls` available at www.excelbreakthrough.com.)

Assume we have the exact same problem as in the previous example, but now we have to look up hundreds or thousands of rows instead of just 23. How long would that take? Suppose it takes 20 seconds on average to manually transpose totals for each required title. Doing 500 titles would take almost three hours, and that assumes we can keep an even keel and not need a break or get frustrated. Even if it took only 10 seconds *on average* for each one, *and* we could keep that pace, it will still take at least 80 minutes. But could we do one every 10 seconds? Could we do one every 20 seconds? What if we averaged one every 30 seconds? Processing just 500 would take over four hours. Yikes!

So let's just assume we still have to process only 23 rows, but in addition to the Media Spending and Product Sales tables we are given one more: that Translation Table mentioned at the end of the last problem that is pictured below:

	A	B
1	**Media Brands**	**Products**
2	MICROSELLER ADSPY DEF SW	Ad-Spy Defense
3	BIG FOUR CORP AUDIT SUITE DLX SW	Audit Deluxe
4	BIG FOUR CORP ADT STE PRO SW	Audit Pro
5	BIG FOUR CORP STNDRD AUDIT	Audit Standard
6	TECHWERKZ SOFTWARE BENCHMARK BASIC	Benchmark Tools Basic
7	TECHWERKZ SOFTWARE BENCHMARK PRO	Benchmark Tools Pro
8	OMNIWEB BROWSER SW	Browser Central
9	HACKERASSIST CORP CODE CRUNCH SW	Code Cruncher
10	TECHWERKZ SOFTWARE DISK SUITE SW	Disk Suite
11	LEARN-TECH INC MATH WIZ	Math Wizard
12	MICROSELLER OFFICE SUITE BASIC SW	Office Tools Basic
13	MICROSELLER ELITE TOOLS OFFICE SW	Office Tools Elite
14	MICROSELLER OFFICE PLS TLS SW	Office Tools Plus
15	MICROSELLER OFFICE PRO TLS SW	Office Tools Professional
16	OMNIWEB PHOTO DLX SW	Photo Deluxe
17	OMNIWEB PHOTO BASIC SW	Photo Organizer
18	MICROSELLER PRES SPIF TOOLS	Presentation Spiffer
19	BIG FOUR CORP BUNDLE PROD	Productivity Bundle
20	LOCKNROCK SECURITY SUITE SW	Security Suite
21	MICROSELLER GRID TOOLS	Speadsheet Tools
22	LEARN-TECH INC SPEL CHLLENGE	Spelling Challenge
23	LOCKNROCK VIRUS BEG SW	Virus Begone

Using the above translation table, how could we use no serious manual effort to fill in the Media Spend totals in the Product Sales table?

Remember, although we are still only transposing data for 23 rows in the Product Sales table in this problem, keep imagining what manually processing thousands of rows would be like using the method in the last problem. Yeah, you don't want to do that or even have to pay someone to do all that manual work. Yechh!

The Solution

The solution now includes a PivotTable and the VLOOKUP formula. If this already feels "too complicated" then absolutely do not stop reading and parsing through the example because if it feels "too complicated," it simply means seeing it through will cause a breakthrough in your ability to use Excel. Ready? Here we go:

1. Create a PivotTable of all the data in the Media Spending table:
    a. Select any cell in the table.
    b. Alt–D–P to launch the PivotTable wizard.
    c. Make sure to create the PivotTable on a new sheet. Here is what it will look like:

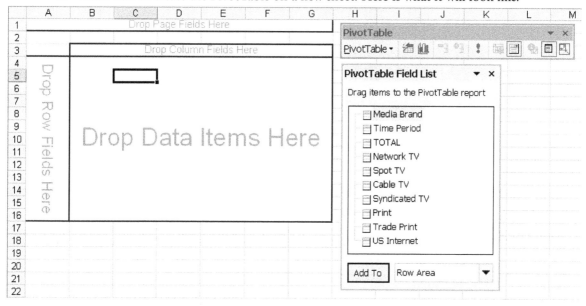

2. Populate the PivotTable as follows:
    a. From the PivotTable Field List, drag the "Media Brand" field to where it says "Drop Row Fields Here" in the table, i.e., anywhere in the range A4:A16 shown in the image in step 1. The result will look like the screenshot below.

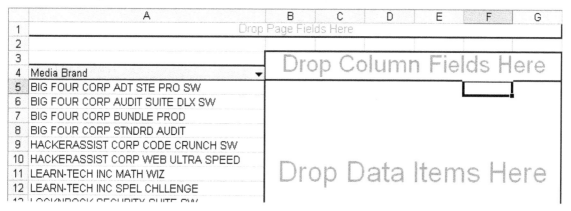

b.   From the PivotTable Field List drag the "TOTAL" field to where it says "Drop Data Items Here" in the table, i.e., anywhere in the range B5:G26 as shown in the image in step 2a above. The result is as shown below.

1	Drop Page Fields Here
2	
3	Sum of TOTAL
4	Media Brand ▼ Total
5	BIG FOUR CORP ADT STE PRO SW — 16294.9
6	BIG FOUR CORP AUDIT SUITE DLX SW — 8710.8
7	BIG FOUR CORP BUNDLE PROD — 5855.5
8	BIG FOUR CORP STNDRD AUDIT — 6544.5
9	HACKERASSIST CORP CODE CRUNCH SW — 11369.7
10	HACKERASSIST CORP WEB ULTRA SPEED — 9432
11	LEARN-TECH INC MATH WIZ — 13085.2
12	LEARN-TECH INC SPEL CHLLENGE — 12157.6
13	LOCKNROCK SECURITY SUITE SW — 6877.2
14	LOCKNROCK VIRUS BEG SW — 8572.6
15	MICROSELLER ADSPY DEF SW — 5050
16	MICROSELLER ELITE TOOLS OFFICE SW — 15726.7
17	MICROSELLER GRID TOOLS — 4271.7
18	MICROSELLER OFFICE PLS TLS SW — 6642.6
19	MICROSELLER OFFICE PRO TLS SW — 20457.6
20	MICROSELLER OFFICE SUITE BASIC SW — 23353.4
21	MICROSELLER PRES SPIF TOOLS — 18283
22	OMNIWEB BROWSER SW — 13739.6
23	OMNIWEB PHOTO DLX SW — 13937.6
24	TECHWERKZ SOFTWARE BENCHMARK BASIC — 9569.1
25	TECHWERKZ SOFTWARE DISK SUITE SW — 16960.9
26	Grand Total — 246892.2

c.   From the PivotTable Field List drag the "Network TV" field to where the "Total Field" is, i.e., anywhere in B4:B26 as shown in the image in step 2b above. The result follows.

1	Drop Page Fields Here		
2			
3	Media Brand ▼	Data ▼	Total
4	BIG FOUR CORP ADT STE PRO SW	Sum of TOTAL	16294.9
5		Count of Network TV	7
6	BIG FOUR CORP AUDIT SUITE DLX SW	Sum of TOTAL	8710.8
7		Count of Network TV	4
8	BIG FOUR CORP BUNDLE PROD	Sum of TOTAL	5855.5
9		Count of Network TV	2
10	BIG FOUR CORP STNDRD AUDIT	Sum of TOTAL	6544.5

d.   Notice "TOTAL" and "Network TV" are stacked and the count of "Network TV" is shown rather than the sum. To fix "stacking" issue, drag the Data header in B3 to C3:

1	Drop Page Fields Here		
2			
3		Data ▼	
4	Media Brand ▼	Sum of TOTAL	Count of Network TV
5	BIG FOUR CORP ADT STE PRO SW	16294.9	7
6	BIG FOUR CORP AUDIT SUITE DLX SW	8710.8	4
7	BIG FOUR CORP BUNDLE PROD	5855.5	2
8	BIG FOUR CORP STNDRD AUDIT	6544.5	3
9	HACKERASSIST CORP CODE CRUNCH SW	11369.7	4
10	HACKERASSIST CORP WEB ULTRA SPEED	9432	3
11	LEARN-TECH INC MATH WIZ	13085.2	6
12	LEARN-TECH INC SPEL CHLLENGE	12157.6	4
13	LOCKNROCK SECURITY SUITE SW	6877.2	3

e. With our table as shown in the previous image, we need to fix the "count" issue.

    i.   Right click the mouse in C4 (where it says "Count of Network TV").

    ii. Select Field Settings.

    iii. Pick Sum and hit OK.

f. Now drag and drop the rest of the Media Spending fields from the PivotTable Field List to the data section of the PivotTable. You may have to manually fix columns that display "Count of" instead of "Sum of."

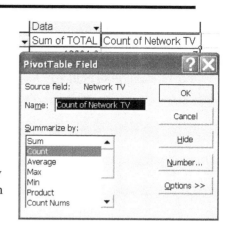

At this point our PivotTable should look like the following:

Media Brand	Sum of TOTAL	Sum of Network TV	Sum of Spot TV	Sum of Cable TV	Sum of Syndicated TV	Sum of Print	Sum of Trade Print	Sum of US Internet
BIG FOUR CORP ADT STE PRO SW	16294.9	3520	146	8130.3	212.2	1400.5	2653.6	232.3
BIG FOUR CORP AUDIT SUITE DLX SW	8710.8	1090.6	0.5	6217.8	5		1327.8	69.1
BIG FOUR CORP BUNDLE PROD	5855.5	191	1	4322.8	6.2	451.5	817.3	65.7
BIG FOUR CORP STNDRD AUDIT	6544.5	1005.2	16.1	3737.9	6.6	336.8	1270.6	171.3
HACKERASSIST CORP CODE CRUNCH SW	11369.7	2833.9	8.7	5049.9		2096.1	936.1	445
HACKERASSIST CORP WEB ULTRA SPEED	9432	2397.5	64	4063.9		735	555.2	1616.4
LEARN-TECH INC MATH WIZ	13085.2	2960	72.2	7181.8			1680.2	1191
LEARN-TECH INC SPEL CHLLENGE	12157.6	2718.9	62	6008.1	107.8	718.6	1564.4	977.8
LOCKNROCK SECURITY SUITE SW	6877.2	2414.2	36.3	3474.6	112.9	348	340.3	150.9
LOCKNROCK VIRUS BEG SW	8572.6	1587	91.5	2806.9	86.2	1046.1	2709.8	245.1
MICROSELLER ADSPY DEF SW	5050	2639.8	212.7	693.7	40.2	851.7	506.9	105
MICROSELLER ELITE TOOLS OFFICE SW	15726.7	1959.8	5.2	9466.6	6.9	1098.5	1608.7	1581
MICROSELLER GRID TOOLS	4271.7	571.3	126.4	2751.4		244	354	224.6
MICROSELLER OFFICE PLS TLS SW	6642.6	929.3	259.7	4370.6	13	158.4	577.4	334.2
MICROSELLER OFFICE PRO TLS SW	20457.6	8578.6	16.5	7813.2	13.8	1883.2	1701.4	450.9
MICROSELLER OFFICE SUITE BASIC SW	23353.4	6487.1	46.4	13147.6	12.4	2178.3	332.2	1149.4
MICROSELLER PRES SPIF TOOLS	18283	5126.7	358.8	10091.2	117.8	329.2	1241.1	1018.2
OMNIWEB BROWSER SW	13739.6	6246.5	8.3	5568.2	69.7	373.8	976.6	496.5
OMNIWEB PHOTO DLX SW	13937.6	2945.9	15.8	9253.4		512	632.7	577.8
TECHWERKZ SOFTWARE BENCHMARK BASIC	9569.1	1112.9	177.2	4664	160.8	1216.4	441.6	1796.2
TECHWERKZ SOFTWARE DISK SUITE SW	16960.9	1621.3	189.7	8918.9	25.1	2406.7	1059.1	2740.1
Grand Total	246892.2	58937.5	1915	127732.8	996.6	18384.8	23287	15638.5

The above PivotTable shows total Media Type by Media Brands for all the months summed up.

3. Still working with our PivotTable …

    a. Insert a blank column to the left of the PivotTable (thus the blank column will be A).

    b. In A5 enter this formula:

    =VLOOKUP(B5,'Translation Table'!A:B,2,FALSE)

    Fill this formula down to the bottom of the PivotTable chart.

    c. Remember, what if we had 500 Media Brands? Even though this example only has 21 rows that need to be filled, we still use Control Method.

    Now we have the Sales brand names mapped to Media Spend brand names on the same page as the monthly totals for each media spend category for each brand. Yes that was a mouthful, so read it again.

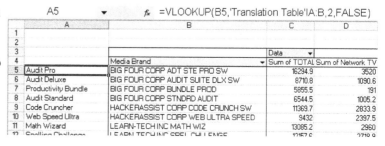

4. To get the Media Spend totals onto the Product Sales sheet, we do one final VLOOKUP formula that uses fixed ranges. But we are going to do it step by step to reinforce your learning of how absolute and relative cell references work.
    a. On the Product Sales sheet in D2 enter the following formula:

    =VLOOKUP(A2, PivotTable!A:J,3,false)

    | E2 | ▼ | | *fx* | =VLOOKUP(A2,PivotTable!A:J,3,FALSE) |

	A	B	C	D	E
1	Product	Total Revenues	Units Sold	Average Sales Price	TOTAL
2	Ad-Spy Defense	$35,565,177	1,425,312	$24.95	5050
3	Audit Deluxe	$46,529,526	1,346,103	$34.57	

    b. Fill this formula (use Control Method!) over to L2. Notice in the image below that the result is #N/A in F2:L2. We need to fix the references so when dragging formulas to the right on this sheet won't produce these errors.

E	F	G	H	I	J	K	L
TOTAL	Network TV	Spot TV	Cable TV	Syndicat ed TV	Print	Trade Print	US Internet
5050	#N/A	#N/A	#N/A	#N/A	#N/A	#N/A	#N/A

5. Fix the references:
    a. Insert a blank row along the top of the Product Sales table.

	A	B	C	D	E	F	G
1							
2	Product	Total Revenues	Units Sold	Average Sales Price	TOTAL	Network TV	Spot
3	Ad-Spy Defense	$35,565,177	1,425,312	$24.95	5050	#N/A	#N/

    b. Now we will enter some values in E1 through L1.
        i.   In F1 enter the value 3.
        ii. In G1 enter the formula =E1+1.
        iii. Select F2. Ctrl+Right to instantly select L2. Up to select L1.
        iv. Ctrl+Shift+Right to highlight F1:L1. Ctrl+R to fill the formulas out to L1. (Remember, that's Ctrl+R and NOT Ctrl+Right.)

fx	=K1+1										
B	C	D	E	F	G	H	I	J	K	L	
			3	4	5	6	7	8	9	10	
Total Revenues	Units Sold	Average Sales Price	TOTAL	Network TV	Spot TV	Cable TV	Syndicat ed TV	Print	Trade Print	US Internet	

    c. Now we will fix the VLOOKUP formula in F3. Compare F3 to the formula in E3. Notice F3 is looking up B3 in the PiviotTable. That doesn't make sense. This happened because the column A reference was not fixed when we dragged it over. To fix this, we go back to E3 and change the first field in the formula from A3 to $A3. Thus, we do the following:

i.   Select cell E3.

ii. Hit F2.

iii. Hold down Left until the cursor is by the "A3" in the formula.

iv. Hit the F4 key three times. Here is what the formula will look like:

E3	▼	f_x =VLOOKUP($A3,PivotTable!A:J,3,FALSE)			
	A	B	C	D	E	F
1					3	4
2	Product	Total Revenues	Units Sold	Average Sales Price	TOTAL	Network TV
3	Ad-Spy Defense	$35,565,177	1,425,312	$24.95	5050	#N/A

Note that we want the first reference to be "$A3" because we want the column reference fixed and *not* the row reference. Later in this example we will fill this formula *down* the table and we won't want the row reference to be fixed.

v.   Next, notice that the formula in cell F3 is looking up data from columns B:K from the PivotTable when it should be looking up data from columns A:J. This problem originated when we dragged the formula: the references shifted when we did not want them to. *Do you see a pattern here?*

Select cell E3 again and change the second field in the formula from PivotTable!A:J to PivotTable!$A:$J.

vi. To do this with the mouse, just click on that A:J part of the formula in the formula bar with the mouse and *then* hit the F4 key.

E3	▼	f_x =VLOOKUP($A3,PivotTable!$A:$J,3,FALSE)			
	A	B	C	D	E	F
1					3	4
2	Product	Total Revenues	Units Sold	Average Sales Price	TOTAL	Network TV
3	Ad-Spy Defense	$35,565,177	1,425,312	$24.95	5050	#N/A

vii. Next, notice that the formula in F3 is also looking up data from the 3rd column of the PivotTable because the column field also has 3 (same as the formula in cell E3). This has to be fixed, too. So, instead of using a fixed column reference number in the 3rd field of the VLOOKUP formula in cell E3, put a reference to cell E1. This is why we put the 3 through 10 in cells E1:L1.

E3	▼	f_x =VLOOKUP($A3,PivotTable!$A:$J,E1,FALSE)			
	A	B	C	D	E	F
1					3	4
2	Product	Total Revenues	Units Sold	Average Sales Price	TOTAL	Network TV
3	Ad-Spy Defense	$35,565,177	1,425,312	$24.95	5050	#N/A

Still reading? You're doing GREAT! Hang in there and keep going!!!

d.   Fill the updated formula in E3 out to L3. Notice this works? No more errors!

fx =VLOOKUP($A3,PivotTable!$A:$J,L1,FALSE)

B	C	D	E	F	G	H	I	J	K	L
			3	4	5	6	7	8	9	10
Total	Units	Average		Network			Syndicat		Trade	US
Revenues	Sold	Sales Price	TOTAL	TV	Spot TV	Cable TV	ed TV	Print	Print	Internet
$35,565,177	1,425,312	$24.95	5050	2639.8	212.7	693.7	40.2	851.7	506.9	105

e.   But that was only the first row of our table. Now we need to fill it *down*. Fill the formula from E3 down to E4. Notice this yields a #REF error in cell E4.

fx =VLOOKUP($A4,PivotTable!$A:$J,E2,FALSE)

B	C	D	E
			3
Total	Units	Average	
Revenues	Sold	Sales Price	TOTAL
$35,565,177	1,425,312	$24.95	5050
$46,529,526	1,346,103	$34.57	#REF!

f.   Notice everything in E4 looks fine except the column index number in the 3rd field. It refers to cell E2 which doesn't make sense. To fix this, go back to E3 and change the third field in the formula from E1 to E$1.

   i.   This makes the column reference un-fixed but the row reference fixed. So when you fill this formula down, the row reference will stay constant while the column reference will be relative.

g.   Now you can fill the formula in E3 into the rest of the empty fields in the table.

   i.   Ctrl+Shift+End should highlight the exact range (double check in case you have extra data somewhere else on the sheet that may throw this off). In any event, you just want to start with cell E3 and then highlight the range E3:L25.

	A	B	C	D	E	F	G	H	I	J	K	L
1					3	4	5	6	7	8	9	10
2	Product	Total Revenues	Units Sold	Average Sales Price	TOTAL	Network TV	Spot TV	Cable TV	Syndicat ed TV	Print	Trade Print	US Internet
3	Ad-Spy Defense	$35,565,177	1,425,312	$24.95	5050	2639.8	212.7	693.7	40.2	851.7	506.9	105
4	Audit Deluxe	$46,529,526	1,346,103	$34.57	8710.8							
5	Audit Pro	$11,589,570	427,025	$27.14								
6	Audit Standard	$25,463,971	957,442	$26.60								
7	Benchmark Tools Basic	$6,519,511	262,932	$24.80								
8	Benchmark Tools Pro	$59,717,367	2,006,864	$29.76								
9	Browser Central	$35,763,262	1,297,332	$27.57								
10	Code Cruncher	$96,826,047	3,148,233	$30.76								
11	Disk Suite	$68,081,550	2,327,837	$29.25								
12	Math Wizard	$28,309,295	1,099,680	$25.74								
13	Office Tools Basic	$36,693,637	1,262,133	$29.07								
14	Office Tools Elite	$173,035,728	5,316,047	$32.55								
15	Office Tools Plus	$54,374,968	1,950,361	$27.88								
16	Office Tools Professional	$54,115,842	1,829,302	$29.58								
17	Photo Deluxe	$16,211,374	697,065	$23.26								
18	Photo Organizer	$131,265,006	4,236,162	$30.99								
19	Presentation Spiffer	$37,183,538	1,342,692	$27.69								
20	Productivity Bundle	$43,274,660	1,426,267	$30.34								
21	Security Suite	$44,687,990	1,564,576	$28.56								
22	Speadsheet Tools	$19,933,796	767,313	$25.98								
23	Spelling Challenge	$20,283,994	741,218	$27.37								
24	Virus Begone	$133,225,801	4,071,017	$32.73								
25	Web Speed Ultra	$132,072,135	4,629,602	$28.53								

ii.   Ctrl+R to Fill right.

iii. Ctrl+D to Fill down.

	A	B	C	D	E	F	G	H	I	J	K	L
1					3	4	5	6	7	8	9	10
2	Product	Total Revenues	Units Sold	Average Sales Price	Network TOTAL	TV	Spot TV	Cable TV	Syndicated TV	Print	Trade Print	US Internet
3	Ad-Spy Defense	$35,565,177	1,425,312	$24.95	5050	2639.8	212.7	693.7	40.2	851.7	506.9	105
4	Audit Deluxe	$46,529,526	1,346,103	$34.57	8710.8	1090.6	0.5	6217.8	5	0	1327.8	69.1
5	Audit Pro	$11,589,570	427,025	$27.14	16294.9	3520	146	8130.3	212.2	1400.5	2653.6	232.3
6	Audit Standard	$25,463,971	957,442	$26.60	6544.5	1005.2	16.1	3737.9	6.6	336.8	1270.6	171.3
7	Benchmark Tools Basic	$6,519,511	262,932	$24.80	9569.1	1112.9	177.2	4664	160.8	1216.4	441.6	1796.2
8	Benchmark Tools Pro	$59,717,367	2,006,864	$29.76	#N/A	#N/A	#N/A	#N/A	#N/A	#N/A	#N/A	#N/A
9	Browser Central	$35,763,262	1,297,332	$27.57	13739.6	6246.5	8.3	5568.2	69.7	373.8	976.6	496.5
10	Code Cruncher	$96,826,047	3,148,233	$30.76	11369.7	2833.9	8.7	5049.9	0	2096.1	936.1	445
11	Disk Suite	$68,081,550	2,327,837	$29.25	16960.9	1621.3	189.7	8918.9	25.1	2406.7	1059.1	2740.1
12	Math Wizard	$28,309,295	1,099,680	$25.74	13085.2	2960	72.2	7181.8	0	0	1680.2	1191
13	Office Tools Basic	$36,693,637	1,262,133	$29.07	23353.4	6487.1	46.4	13147.6	12.4	2178.3	332.2	1149.4
14	Office Tools Elite	$173,035,728	5,316,047	$32.55	15726.7	1959.8	5.2	9466.6	6.9	1098.5	1608.7	1581
15	Office Tools Plus	$54,374,968	1,950,361	$27.88	6642.6	929.3	259.7	4370.6	13	158.4	577.4	334.2
16	Office Tools Professional	$54,115,842	1,829,302	$29.58	20457.6	8578.6	16.5	7813.2	13.8	1883.2	1701.4	450.9
17	Photo Deluxe	$16,211,374	697,065	$23.26	13937.6	2945.9	15.8	9253.4	0	512	632.7	577.8
18	Photo Organizer	$131,265,006	4,236,162	$30.99	#N/A	#N/A	#N/A	#N/A	#N/A	#N/A	#N/A	#N/A
19	Presentation Spiffer	$37,183,538	1,342,692	$27.69	18283	5126.7	358.8	10091.2	117.8	329.2	1241.1	1018.2
20	Productivity Bundle	$43,274,660	1,426,267	$30.34	5855.5	191	1	4322.8	6.2	451.5	817.3	65.7
21	Security Suite	$44,687,990	1,564,576	$28.56	6877.2	2414.2	36.3	3474.6	112.9	348	340.3	150.9
22	Speadsheet Tools	$19,933,796	767,313	$25.98	4271.7	571.3	126.4	2751.4	0	244	354	224.6
23	Spelling Challenge	$20,283,994	741,218	$27.37	12157.6	2718.9	62	6008.1	107.8	718.6	1564.4	977.8
24	Virus Begone	$133,225,801	4,071,017	$32.73	8572.6	1587	91.5	2806.9	86.2	1046.1	2709.8	245.1

6. Notice that all the lookups are complete. Spot check the data to verify the results.

Also notice that in rows **8** and **18** the results are **#N/A** errors. This happened because the products in those rows, Benchmark Tools Pro and Photo Organizer, respectively, were not in the PivotTable because they had no entries in the large Media Spending table. This may happen sometimes when you don't always have matches when using VLOOKUP.

Congratulations! You did it! Or as some of my clients in the video game industry might say, "w00t! u r teh l337 h4x0r!" ("You are the elite hacker!")

Problem 6 – Alternating Row Formats

(This problem uses the file `Alternating Row Formats.xls` available at www.excelbreakthrough.com.)

I had a client who had to set up a list of data records that would be printed and posted on a wall for people in his office to review and write notes on. His list looked like this …

	A	B
1	**Description**	**Comments**
2	Item A	
3	Product 1	
4	Product 2	
5	Item B	
6	Product 3	
7	Item C	
8	Item D	
9	Product 4	
10	Prodcut 5	
11	Product 5	
12	Prodcut 6	
13	Product 6	
14	Prodcut 7	
15	Product 7	
16	Prodcut 8	
17	Product 8	
18	Prodcut 9	
19	Product 9	
20	Prodcut 10	
21	Item E	
22	Item F	
23	Item G	

… and he wanted it to look like this:

	A	B
1	**Description**	**Comments**
2	Item A	
3	Product 1	
4	Product 2	
5	Item B	
6	Product 3	
7	Item C	
8	Item D	
9	Product 4	
10	Prodcut 5	
11	Product 5	
12	Prodcut 6	
13	Product 6	
14	Prodcut 7	
15	Product 7	
16	Prodcut 8	
17	Product 8	
18	Prodcut 9	
19	Product 9	
20	Prodcut 10	
21	Item E	
22	Item F	
23	Item G	

How could we do this quickly? His table had 400 rows, but for this example will keep it simple with just 22 rows. Here are a few solutions:

Solution #1

(This solution uses the tab "Original no text formats" in the file `Alternating Row Formats.xls` available at www.excelbreakthrough.com.)

This was my client's initial solution:

1. Select A1:B1 and give it a Fill Color of Gray 40%.

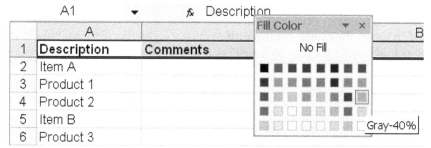

2. Select the first data record (A2:B2) and give it a Fill Color of Gray 25%.

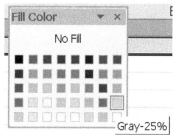

3. Select the second data record (A3:B3) and give it a Fill Color of White.

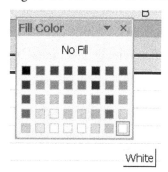

At this point our table looks like the following:

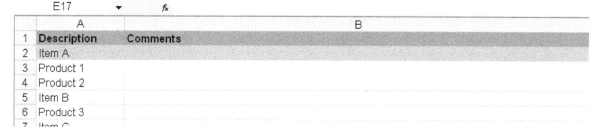

Notice that the White cell shading in A3:B3 is only visually detectable because the borders around those cells are white, making it look like the cells bleed into the cells around it.

4. Highlight the first two records in the range **A2:B4**.

5. Hit the Format Painter button on the Standard toolbar.

6.   Use the mouse to highlight exactly the unformatted remaining rows of the table. When my client did this, he had nearly 400 additional rows to highlight. (3 through 400).

   a.   To make this work, you have to manually highlight all the rows with the mouse first without letting go of the mouse button. This is not an impossible task at all, but it can be a bit tedious given the mouse work involved, especially when we need to highlight down to row 400. If you pull the mouse pointer down, Excel scrolls way too fast.

7.   Let go of the mouse button.

This worked. It wasn't the easiest dealing with manually highlighting such a long range using the mouse, but as I said above it works. A much faster approach would have been as follows:

Solution #2

1.   Repeat steps 1 through 4 above.

2.   Instead of using only the mouse to paint the formats, add in some handy Control Method.

   a.   Select A2.
   b.   Shift+Left.
   c.   Shift+Down.
   d.   Hit Format Painter button with mouse.
   e.   Ctrl+Shift+Down.

That's it! If you recall, you can use Control Method with Format Painter.

Anyway, my client did his solution above and at first I was glad it didn't take him too long, but when I looked closer I noticed that his method overwrote the **bold** and *italics* formats of some of the rows down the list. Out of his nearly 400 rows, about 10% had descriptions in **bold** to identify new items on the list from the last time this was done. Another 5% had descriptions in *italics* with old items that would be gone from the list the next time the list was printed. When he did the simple Format Painter technique above, the plain formatting of the text in the first two rows overrode the text formatting in the rest of the list. So all the problematic **bold** and *italics* rows were gone.

I pointed this problem out to my client who quickly exclaimed, "$#%! I have to do this over line by line!?" Thankfully I was there and showed him this simple *Excel Breakthrough* method:

Solution #3

(This solution uses the tab "Original with text formats" in the `Alternating Row Formats.xls` file available at www. excelbreakthrough.com.)

Now imagine that our example table of 22 rows to be formatted looks like the one at right.

To preserve the existing text formats and only update the Fill Colors in this scenario, use this method:

1.   Insert 2 columns to the left of the table. I suggest using the following:

   a.   Select anywhere in column A.

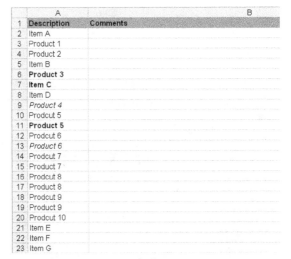

	A	B
1	**Description**	Comments
2	Item A	
3	Product 1	
4	Product 2	
5	Item B	
6	**Product 3**	
7	**Item C**	
8	Item D	
9	*Product 4*	
10	Prodcut 5	
11	**Product 5**	
12	Prodcut 6	
13	*Product 6*	
14	Prodcut 7	
15	Product 7	
16	Prodcut 8	
17	Product 8	
18	Prodcut 9	
19	Product 9	
20	Prodcut 10	
21	Item E	
22	Item F	
23	Item G	

    b.   Ctrl+Space to highlight column A.

    c.   Hit Menu–I *twice* to insert two empty columns.

2.   In cell A1 type "Rank" and in cell B1 type "Color" as shown:

	A	B	C
1	Rank	Color	**Description**
2			Item A
3			Product 1
4			Product 2
5			Item B

3.   In cell A2 enter value of 1.

4.   In cell A3 enter formula =A2+1.

5.   In cell B2 enter value of 1.

6.   In cell B3 enter value of 2.

A3 ▼ f_x =A2+1

	A	B	C
1	Rank	Color	**Description**
2	1	1	Item A
3	2	2	Product 1

7.   Select C1.

8.   Ctrl+Down to get to the end of the list.

9.   Ctrl+Left to select bottom of table in column A.

10. Ctrl+Shift+Up to highlight up to A3.

11. Ctrl+D to Fill down.

12. Ctrl+C to copy.

13. ALT–E–S–V–Enter to paste values. *Do not miss this step or else this process will not work!*

14. Now select B2:B3.

15. Ctrl+C to copy.

	A	B	C
1	Rank	Color	**Description**
2	1	1	Item A
3	2	2	Product 1
4	3		Product 2

16. However you want, highlight the range B4:B23. I suggest:

    a.   Select C2.

    b.   Ctrl+Down to get to the bottom of the table in column C.

    c.   Select bottom of table in column B.

    d.   Ctrl+Shift+Up. This will select B3:B23.

   e.   Shift+Down to deselect B3. You are left with B4:B23.

17. Ctrl+V to paste and hit Esc to exit cut/copy/paste mode.

18. Ctrl+H select A1.

	A	B	
1	Rank	Color	
2	1	1	
3	2	2	P
4	3		P
5	4		
6	5		F
7	6		
8	7		
9	8		
10	9		P
11	10		F
12	11		F
13	12		
14	13		F
15	14		F
16	15		F
17	16		F
18	17		F
19	18		F
20	19		F
21	20		
22	21		
23	22		

19. ALT–D–S to bring up the Sort dialog box and sort on Color ascending.

	A	B	C	
1	Rank	Color	**Description**	**Comments**
2	1	1	Item A	
3	3	1	Product 2	
4	5	1	**Product 3**	
5	7	1	Item D	
6	9	1	Prodcut 5	
7	11	1	Prodcut 6	
8	13	1	Prodcut 7	
9	15	1	Prodcut 8	
10	17	1	Prodcut 9	
11	19	1	Prodcut 10	
12	21	1	Item F	
13	2	2	Product 1	
14	4	2	Item B	
15	6	2	**Item C**	
16	8	2	*Product 4*	
17	10	2	**Product 5**	
18	12	2	*Product 6*	
19	14	2	Product 7	
20	16	2	Product 8	
21	18	2	Product 9	
22	20	2	Item E	
23	22	2	Item G	

At this point we can now apply our first color (Gray -25%) to all rows with 1 as the color value and our second color (White) to all rows with 2 as the color value.

When my client and I went through this process on his list with over 400 rows, we used Find to get the first row with color 2 because it was far enough down that we would have to scroll for a bit. Even though the example in this book only has 22 rows to color, we're going to use the Find function just the same to illustrate.

20. Select B1.

21. Ctrl+Spacebar to select all of column B.

22. Ctrl+F to open the Find dialog box. Search for value 2.

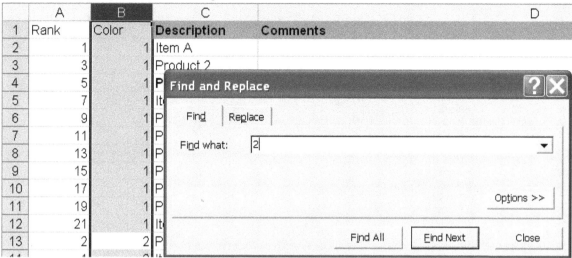

23. Hit the Left Arrow key once to deselect all of column B but still have row 13 selected. (Row 13 is the start of the color 2 rows in this example.)

24. Ctrl+Shift to select all of row 13.

25. Ctrl+Shift+Down to highlight all rows with the value 2 in column B.

26. Apply the White cell shading as shown above.

27. Now using a similar process, select only the rows with the value 1 in column B.

28. Apply Gray 25% as show above.

At this point you will notice that columns E, F, G, etc. all the way out to the end of the spreadsheet have highlight. If you don't want this, as my client did not want, simply do the following:

29. Select E1.

30. Ctrl+Spacebar to highlight all of column E.

31. Ctrl+Shift+Right to expand the selection to include all columns to the right of E.

32. Select "No Fill" as shown:

And here is our table as it stands now:

	A	B	C	D
1	Rank	Color	**Description**	Comments
2	1	1	Item A	
3	3	1	Product 2	
4	5	1	**Product 3**	
5	7	1	Item D	
6	9	1	Prodcut 5	
7	11	1	Prodcut 6	
8	13	1	Prodcut 7	
9	15	1	Prodcut 8	
10	17	1	Prodcut 9	
11	19	1	Prodcut 10	
12	21	1	Item F	
13	2	2	Product 1	
14	4	2	Item B	
15	6	2	**Item C**	
16	8	2	*Product 4*	
17	10	2	**Product 5**	
18	12	2	*Product 6*	
19	14	2	Product 7	
20	16	2	Product 8	
21	18	2	Product 9	
22	20	2	Item E	
23	22	2	Item G	

Next we need to put the table back in its original sequence.

33. Ctrl+Home to select A1.

34. ALT–D–S to open the Sort dialog box.
    a.   Sort on Rank ascending.

The table will now be sorted correctly but we still need to delete columns A and B.

35. Use Ctrl+Spacebar to highlight columns A and B.

36. Menu–D to delete columns A and B.

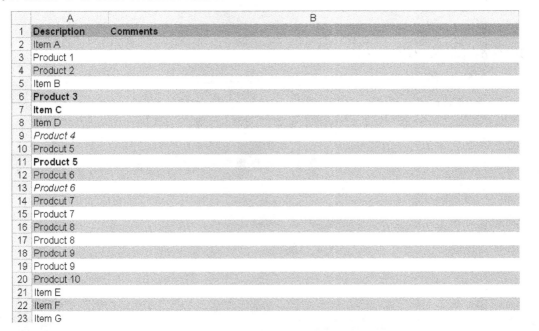

	A	B
1	**Description**	Comments
2	Item A	
3	Product 1	
4	Product 2	
5	Item B	
6	**Product 3**	
7	**Item C**	
8	Item D	
9	*Product 4*	
10	Prodcut 5	
11	**Product 5**	
12	Prodcut 6	
13	*Product 6*	
14	Prodcut 7	
15	Product 7	
16	Prodcut 8	
17	Product 8	
18	Prodcut 9	
19	Product 9	
20	Prodcut 10	
21	Item E	
22	Item F	
23	Item G	

Problem 7 – Managing Yourself

(This example uses the sample file Managing Yoursef.xls available at www.excelbreakthrough.com.)

One of my clients had a long list (over 5,500 rows) in a simple table of products sold by the many different manufacturers in her industry with total unit sales for each over a long time period. While we can't see all 5,500+ rows in one screenshot, here is the top of the list showing the first 17 rows:

	A	B
1	**Product Name**	**Unit Sales**
2	Product 1	95,452
3	Product 2	68,173
4	Product 3	107,416
5	Product 4	169,593
6	Product 5	368,381
7	Product 6	72,733
8	Product 7	44,483
9	Product 8	197,049
10	Product 9	148,717
11	Product 10	66,848
12	Product 11	40,350
13	Product 12	57,871
14	Product 13	46,662
15	Product 14	52,508
16	Product 15	136,228
17	Product 16	111,730
18	Product 17	93,913

The list went on and on and scattered through the list with no particular logic were about 150 products that had Unit Sales greater than 1,000,000.

Her boss wanted her to write a brief comment in column C for only the products that sold over 1,000,000 units that might briefly explain their success.

But there were catches:

- The list was already in a specific order, grouped by manufacturer and her boss wanted her to leave it that way when she sent it back to him with only her comments added.
- For the products that sold over 1,000,000 units, the explanation for the sales success was often related to the other products the manufacturer sold, so the sequence really had to stay intact as she processed it.

When her boss was explaining this to her in her office, her hands curled into fists under her desk and her jaw hardened into stone. If "suppressed rage" had a face it would have been hers in that moment. How do I know? I was sitting five feet away when her boss gave her this assignment. He hadn't even noticed I was there when he barged in, dumped this on her and then left for an offsite meeting. Because he had made it her top priority, her work with me had to wait, even though her company was paying for my time and the output of our project. After he left the room she shut her door and said, "This is going to take me forever. Crap like this makes me want to quit." While there was nothing I could do about her boss giving her such work, I knew I could make it easier to do the assignment and at least not let it ruin her day.

So what happened? How did she handle the request?

Her approach was to visually scan down the list, find rows where the units were greater than 1,000,000 and insert her comment in the blank cell in that row to the right of the list.

For a short list, manually processing is the fastest solution. For a long list of 5,500+ rows it is possibly "doable" but for each row that needed a comment she would have to use more than a trivial amount of mental energy to pick it out from the others. It would be draining because as she scanned down the list she would have to do a lot of mouse clicking and mouse movement back and forth between the scroll bar on the right and the cells in the table. Or she could simply use the Down Arrow, but that would not eliminate using mental energy to pick out the required cells and it would be slow to go through all 5,500+ rows like that.

And she knew it would be draining, too. "You're good with Excel," she said to me, "how can I do this without going crazy?"

"Don't worry," I said, "I've got you covered."

The Solution

1. Insert a Freeze Pane between rows 1 and 2, so that the headers in row 1 will always be visible:
    a. Select A2.
    b. Alt–W–F to insert the Freeze Pane.

	A	B
1	**Product Name**	**Unit Sales**
2	Product 1	95,452
3	Product 2	68,173
4	Product 3	107,416

2. Select C1 and start typing the following formula:

    =countif(

SUMIF	▾ ✕ ✓ *fx*	=countif(		
	A	B	C	D
1	**Product Name**	**Unit Sales**	=countif(	
2	Product 1	95,452	COUNTIF(**range**, criteria)	

    As you should know by now, Excel prompts us for a criteria.

3. Use the Arrow keys to select cell B2:

SUMIF	▾ ✕ ✓ *fx*	=countif(B2		
	A	B	C	D
1	**Product Name**	**Unit Sales**	=countif(B2	
2	Product 1	95,452	COUNTIF(**range**, criteria)	

4. Next we need to get the entire range from B2 down to the bottom of the list:
    a. Ctrl+Shit+Down:

SUMIF	▾ ✕ ✓ *fx*	=countif(B2:B5515		
	A	B	C	D
1	**Product Name**	**Unit Sales**	=countif(B2:B5515	
5506	Product 5505	541	COUNTIF(**range**, criteria)	
5507	Product 5506	44,009		
5508	Product 5507	91,534		
5509	Product 5508	222,827		
5510	Product 5509	30,074		
5511	Product 5510	111,049		
5512	Product 5511	67,141		
5513	Product 5512	589,644		
5514	Product 5513	14,678		
5515	Product 5514	25,395		

b. Hit the Comma to activate the next field in the formula as shown below:

SUMIF	▼ ✕ ✓ *fx* =countif(B2:B5515,		
A	B	C	D
1 Product Name	Unit Sales	=countif(B2:B5515,	
5506 Product 5505	541	COUNTIF(range, **criteria**)	

5. For the criteria, type the following, including the double quotation marks as shown:

">1000000"

SUMIF	▼ ✕ ✓ *fx* =countif(B2:B5515,">1000000")			
A	B	C	D	E
1 Product Name	Unit Sales	=countif(B2:B5515,">1000000")		
5506 Product 5505	541			

... and of course hit enter. This shows us how many products have Unit Sales greater than 1,000,000:

C1	▼	*fx* =COUNTIF(B2:B5515,">1000000")	
A	B	C	D
1 Product Name	Unit Sales	154	
2 Product 1	95,452		

We can see that we have 154 rows to enter comments for.

6. Because we need to keep the rows in order as we process them we cannot simply sort the list by Unit Sales to isolate them at one end of the list. We also need a faster way to locate them and type in comments next to them in column C than by using visual inspection. Here's what we do, and don't worry if you have never seen this before:
   a. Select C2 and enter the formula as shown:

=if(B2>1000000,1,0)

C2	▼	*fx* =IF(B2>1000000,1,0)	
A	B	C	D
1 Product Name	Unit Sales	154	
2 Product 1	95,452	0	
3 Product 2	68,173		

   b. Select B2.
   c. Ctrl+Down to select the last row in the list in column B.
   d. Select C5515, which is easily done using the Right Arrow key!

A	B	C
1 Product Name	Unit Sales	154
5509 Product 5508	222,827	
5510 Product 5509	30,074	
5511 Product 5510	111,049	
5512 Product 5511	67,141	
5513 Product 5512	589,644	
5514 Product 5513	14,678	
5515 Product 5514	25,395	

e.   Ctrl+Shift+Up:

	A	B	C	D
1	**Product Name**	**Unit Sales**	154	
2	Product 1	95,452	0	
3	Product 2	68,173		
4	Product 3	107,416		
5	Product 4	169,593		
6	Product 5	368,381		
7	Product 6	72,733		
8	Product 7	44,483		
9	Product 8	107,040		

f.   Ctrl+D to copy the formula in C2 all the way down to C5515.

Now that we have the formulas down to the bottom of the range, we need to copy and paste the values in place. Still with C2:C5515 highlighted as shown above, keep going …

C5515   ▼   *fx*   =IF(B5515>1000000,1,0)

	A	B	C	D
1	**Product Name**	**Unit Sales**	154	
2	Product 1	95,452	0	
3	Product 2	68,173	0	
4	Product 3	107,416	0	
5	Product 4	169,593	0	
6	Product 5	368,381	0	
7	Product 6	72,733	0	
8	Product 7	44,483	0	
9	Product 8	107,040	0	

g.   Ctrl+C to copy C2:C5515.

h.   Alt–E–S–V–Enter to paste the values in place. Now when we select any of those cells in that range instead of seeing the formula we see the value 1 or 0. But we are only interested in rows where the value is 1.

i.   Highlight all of C2:C5515.

j.   Ctrl+H to open the Find/Replace dialog.

   i.   In the "Find what:" field enter 0:

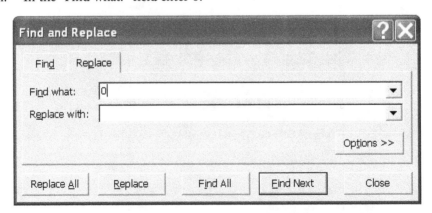

ii.   Alt–A to select Replace All as shown above. We'll see the following message:

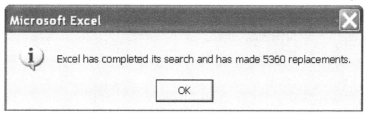

Notice all the 0 values have gone away.

k.   We are almost ready to enter comments. But before we do we want to add a little visual aid.

i.   Select cell **D1** and enter the following formula:

=SUM(C2:C5515)/C1

ii.   Still with **D1** selected, hit the percentage format button on the format toolbar:

D1	▼	*fx*	=SUM(C2:C5515)/C1	
	A	B	C	D	E
1	**Product Name**	**Unit Sales**	154	100%	
2	Product 1	95,452			

The value displayed in D1 is 100% of cells that still need a comment. Why would we care? Keep reading!

7.   Now we've made it to the part where we enter comments. We start by selecting **C2** as shown below. And if you are following along with the included example file, you immediately see that the first cell requiring a comment is somewhere down the list.

	A	B	C	D
1	**Product Name**	**Unit Sales**	154	100%
2	Product 1	95,452		
3	Product 2	68,173		
4	Product 3	107,416		
5	Product 4	169,593		
6	Product 5	368,381		
7	Product 6	72,733		

a.   To get to that first cell needing a comment, we start with **C2** selected as shown above and hit Ctrl+Down. This takes us to **C155**:

	A	B	C	D
1	**Product Name**	**Unit Sales**	154	100%
149	Product 148	6,203		
150	Product 149	107,849		
151	Product 150	143,925		
152	Product 151	51,515		
153	Product 152	827,772		
154	Product 153	23,862		
155	Product 154	1,552,273	1	
156	Product 155	120,710		

b. Type in a comment in C155.

	A	B	C	D
1	**Product Name**	**Unit Sales**	154	99%
149	Product 148	6,203		
150	Product 149	107,849		
151	Product 150	143,925		
152	Product 151	51,515		
153	Product 152	827,772		
154	Product 153	23,862		
155	Product 154	1,552,273	First comment	
156	Product 155	120,710		

Notice that the value in D1 is now less than 100%. That's because the sum of the values in C2:C5515 is now less than 154, which was the original amount of cells needing comments. And recall that in D1 our formula is:

=SUM(C2:C5515)/C1

...where C1 is the total number or cells in column B with a value greater than 1,000,000.

c. Still with C155 selected, hit Ctrl+Down again. This takes us to C237:

	A	B	C	D
1	**Product Name**	**Unit Sales**	154	99%
234	Product 233	69,038		
235	Product 234	131,283		
236	Product 235	61,126		
237	Product 236	1,298,204	1	
238	Product 237	1,404,374	1	
239	Product 238	4,544		

d. Enter a comment in C237, and then another one in C238:

C238   ▼   *fx* Third comment

	A	B	C	D
1	**Product Name**	**Unit Sales**	154	98%
234	Product 233	69,038		
235	Product 234	131,283		
236	Product 235	61,126		
237	Product 236	1,298,204	Second comment	
238	Product 237	1,404,374	Third comment	
239	Product 238	4,544		

Notice now that D1 has dropped to 98%. We could show more decimals if we wanted to, but this illustrates the point.

As we keep using Ctrl+Down to get to the next cell with a 1 value in column C and enter a comment, the value in D1 goes toward 0%.

So as we process each cell in the list, we get **visual feedback** on our progress which helps keep us motivated to get to zero.

My client couldn't believe it. "I would have never have thought to have done that," she said, "and I'm a little embarrassed. I'm a marketing director who deals with financial and budget data all the time. I should know how to use Excel better."

I nodded, understanding her perspective. "But are you really paid for your knowledge of Excel data processing or for your experience as a marketing strategist and team leader?"

She thought about it a moment and finally smiled again. "Thanks," she said.

The real lesson in this problem was to use just a bit of visual feedback (in this case the COUNTIF formula) to help keep us motivated. Initially my client assumed this was an impossible task that would ruin her day, but using just a bit of *Excel Breakthrough* thinking she was able to manage her own thoughts and feelings about her task in Excel and not focus on how bad she felt about the intrusion in her workday.

Appendix A
Full List of Default
Keyboard Shortcuts

The following list of shortcuts comes directly from Microsoft Excel Help included with the software. You can access this any time by hitting the F1 key in Excel to bring up the following:

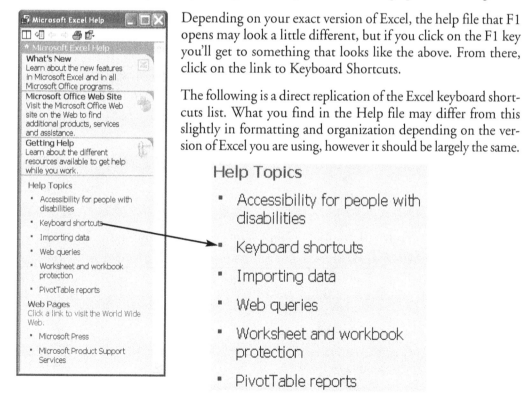

Depending on your exact version of Excel, the help file that F1 opens may look a little different, but if you click on the F1 key you'll get to something that looks like the above. From there, click on the link to Keyboard Shortcuts.

The following is a direct replication of the Excel keyboard shortcuts list. What you find in the Help file may differ from this slightly in formatting and organization depending on the version of Excel you are using, however it should be largely the same.

Keys for Workbooks and Worksheets

Preview and Print:

CTRL+P or CTRL+SHIFT+F12
> Display the Print dialog box.

Use the following keys in print preview (to get to print preview, use Alt–F–V):

Arrow keys
> Move around the page when zoomed in.

PAGE UP or PAGE DOWN
> Move by one page when zoomed out.

CTRL+UP ARROW or CTRL+LEFT ARROW
> Move to the first page when zoomed out.

CTRL+DOWN ARROW or CTRL+RIGHT ARROW
> Move to the last page when zoomed out.

Work with worksheets:

SHIFT+F11 or ALT+SHIFT+F1
> Insert a new worksheet.

CTRL+PAGE DOWN
> Move to the next sheet in the workbook.

CTRL+PAGE UP
> Move to the previous sheet in the workbook.

SHIFT+CTRL+PAGE DOWN
> Select the current and next sheet. To cancel selection of multiple sheets, press
> CTRL+PAGE DOWN or, to select a different sheet, press CTRL+PAGE UP.

SHIFT+CTRL+PAGE UP
> Select the current and previous sheet.

ALT+O H R
> Rename the current sheet (Format menu, Sheet submenu, Rename command).

ALT+E M
> Move or copy the current sheet (Edit menu, Move or Copy Sheet command).

ALT+E L
> Delete the current sheet (Edit menu, Delete Sheet command).

Move and scroll within worksheets:

Arrow keys
> Move one cell up, down, left, or right.

CTRL+Arrow key
> Move to the edge of the current data region.

HOME
> Move to the beginning of the row.

CTRL+HOME
> Move to the beginning of the worksheet.

CTRL+END
> Move to the last cell on the worksheet, in the bottom-most used row of the rightmost used column.

PAGE DOWN
> Move down one screen.

PAGE UP
> Move up one screen.

ALT+PAGE DOWN
> Move one screen to the right.

ALT+PAGE UP
> Move one screen to the left.

F6
> Switch to the next pane in a worksheet that has been split (Window menu, Split command).

SHIFT+F6
> Switch to the previous pane in a worksheet that has been split.

CTRL+BACKSPACE
> Scroll to display the active cell.

F5
> Display the Go To dialog box.

SHIFT+F5
> Display the Find dialog box.

SHIFT+F4
> Repeat the last Find action (same as Find Next).

TAB
> Move between unlocked cells on a protected worksheet.

Move within a selected range:

ENTER
> Move from top to bottom within the selected range.

SHIFT+ENTER
> Move from bottom to top within the selected range.

TAB
> Move from left to right within the selected range. If cells in a single column are selected, move down.

SHIFT+TAB
> Move from right to left within the selected range. If cells in a single column are selected, move up.

CTRL+PERIOD
> Move clockwise to the next corner of the selected range.

CTRL+ALT+RIGHT ARROW
> In nonadjacent selections, switch to the next selection to the right.

CTRL+ALT+LEFT ARROW
> Switch to the next nonadjacent selection to the left.

Move and scroll in End mode:

END appears in the status bar when End mode is selected.

END key
> Turn End mode on or off.

END+Arrow key
> Move by one block of data within a row or column.

END+HOME
> Move to the last cell on the worksheet, in the bottom-most used row of the rightmost used column.

END+ENTER
> Move to the rightmost nonblank cell in the current row. This key sequence does not work if you have turned on transition navigation keys (Tools menu, Options command, Transition tab).

Move and scroll with SCROLL LOCK on:

When you use scrolling keys (such as PAGE UP and PAGE DOWN) with SCROLL LOCK off, cell selection moves the distance you scroll. To scroll without changing which cells are selected, turn on SCROLL LOCK first.

SCROLL LOCK
> Turn SCROLL LOCK on or off.

HOME
> Move to the cell in the upper-left corner of the window.

END
> Move to the cell in the lower-right corner of the window.

UP ARROW or DOWN ARROW
> Scroll one row up or down.

LEFT ARROW or RIGHT ARROW
> Scroll one column left or right.

Keys for Selecting Data and Cells

Select cells, rows and columns, and objects:

CTRL+SPACEBAR
> Select the entire column.

SHIFT+SPACEBAR
> Select the entire row.

CTRL+A
> Select the entire worksheet.

SHIFT+BACKSPACE
> With multiple cells selected, select only the active cell.

CTRL+SHIFT+SPACEBAR
> With an object selected, select all objects on a sheet.

CTRL+6

> Alternate between hiding objects, displaying objects, and displaying placeholders for objects.

Select cells with specific characteristics:

CTRL+SHIFT+* (asterisk)

> Select the current region around the active cell (the data area enclosed by blank rows and blank columns). In a PivotTable report, select the entire PivotTable report.

CTRL+/

> Select the array containing the active cell.

CTRL+SHIFT+O (the letter O)

> Select all cells that contain comments.

CTRL+\

> In a selected row, select the cells that don't match the value in the active cell.

CTRL+SHIFT+|

> In a selected column, select the cells that don't match the value in the active cell.

CTRL+[(opening bracket)

> Select all cells directly referenced by formulas in the selection.

CTRL+SHIFT+{ (opening brace)

> Select all cells directly or indirectly referenced by formulas in the selection.

CTRL+] (closing bracket)

> Select cells that contain formulas that directly reference the active cell.

CTRL+SHIFT+} (closing brace)

> Select cells that contain formulas that directly or indirectly reference the active cell.

ALT+; (semicolon)

> Select the visible cells in the current selection.

Extend a selection:

F8

> Turn extend mode on or off. In extend mode, EXT appears in the status line, and the Arrow keys extend the selection.

SHIFT+F8

> Add another range of cells to the selection; or use the Arrow keys to move to the start of the range you want to add, and then press F8 and the Arrow keys to select the next range.

SHIFT+Arrow key

> Extend the selection by one cell.

CTRL+SHIFT+Arrow key

> Extend the selection to the last nonblank cell in the same column or row as the active cell.

SHIFT+HOME

> Extend the selection to the beginning of the row.

CTRL+SHIFT+HOME

> Extend the selection to the beginning of the worksheet.

CTRL+SHIFT+END
>   Extend the selection to the last used cell on the worksheet (lower-right corner).

SHIFT+PAGE DOWN
>   Extend the selection down one screen.

SHIFT+PAGE UP
>   Extend the selection up one screen.

END+SHIFT+Arrow key
>   Extend the selection to the last nonblank cell in the same column or row as the active cell.

END+SHIFT+HOME
>   Extend the selection to the last used cell on the worksheet (lower-right corner).

END+SHIFT+ENTER
>   Extend the selection to the last cell in the current row. This key sequence does not work if you have turned on transition navigation keys (Tools menu, Options command, Transition tab).

SCROLL LOCK+SHIFT+HOME
>   Extend the selection to the cell in the upper-left corner of the window.

SCROLL LOCK+SHIFT+END
>   Extend the selection to the cell in the lower-right corner of the window.

Keys for Entering, Editing, Formatting, and Calculating

Enter data:

ENTER
>   Complete a cell entry and select the cell below.

ALT+ENTER
>   Start a new line in the same cell.

CTRL+ENTER
>   Fill the selected cell range with the current entry.

SHIFT+ENTER
>   Complete a cell entry and select the previous cell above.

TAB
>   Complete a cell entry and select the next cell to the right.

SHIFT+TAB
>   Complete a cell entry and select the previous cell to the left.

ESC
>   Cancel a cell entry.

Arrow keys
>   Move one character up, down, left, or right.

HOME
>   Move to the beginning of the line.

F4 or CTRL+Y
>   Repeat the last action.

CTRL+SHIFT+F3
>   Create names from row and column labels.

CTRL+D
> Fill down.

CTRL+R
> Fill to the right.

CTRL+F3
> Define a name.

CTRL+K
> Insert a hyperlink.

ENTER (in a cell with a hyperlink)
> Activate a hyperlink.

CTRL+; (semicolon)
> Enter the date.

CTRL+SHIFT+: (colon)
> Enter the time.

ALT+DOWN ARROW
> Display a drop-down list of the values in the current column of a list.

CTRL+Z
> Undo the last action.

Enter special characters:

Press F2 to edit the cell, turn on NUM LOCK, and then press the following keys by using the numeric key pad:

ALT+0162
> Enters the cent character ¢.

ALT+0163
> Enters the pound sterling character £.

ALT+0165
> Enters the yen symbol ¥.

ALT+0128
> Enters the euro symbol .

Enter and calculate formulas:

= (equal sign)
> Start a formula.

F2
> Move the insertion point into the Formula Bar when editing in a cell that is turned off.

BACKSPACE
> In the Formula Bar, delete one character to the left.

ENTER
> Complete a cell entry from the cell or Formula Bar.

CTRL+SHIFT+ENTER
> Enter a formula as an array formula.

ESC
> Cancel an entry in the cell or Formula Bar.

SHIFT+F3
> In a formula, display the Insert Function dialog box.

CTRL+A
> When the insertion point is to the right of a function name in a formula, display the Function Arguments dialog box.

CTRL+SHIFT+A
> When the insertion point is to the right of a function name in a formula, insert the argument names and parentheses.

F3
> Paste a defined name into a formula.

ALT+= (equal sign)
> Insert an AutoSum formula with the SUM function.

CTRL+SHIFT+" (quotation mark)
> Copy the value from the cell above the active cell into the cell or the Formula Bar.

CTRL+' (apostrophe)
> Copies a formula from the cell above the active cell into the cell or the Formula Bar.

CTRL+` (single left quotation mark)
> Alternate between displaying cell values and displaying formulas.

F9
> Calculate all worksheets in all open workbooks.
> When a portion of a formula is selected, calculate the selected portion. You can then press ENTER or CTRL+SHIFT+ENTER (for array formulas) to replace the selected portion with the calculated value.

SHIFT+F9
> Calculate the active worksheet.

CTRL+ALT+F9
> Calculate all worksheets in all open workbooks, regardless of whether they have changed since the last calculation.

CTRL+ALT+SHIFT+F9
> Rechecks dependent formulas and then calculates all cells in all open workbooks, including cells not marked as needing to be calculated.

Edit data:

F2
> Edit the active cell and position the insertion point at the end of the cell contents.

ALT+ENTER
> Start a new line in the same cell.

BACKSPACE
> Edit the active cell and then clear it, or delete the preceding character in the active cell as you edit cell contents.

DELETE
> Delete the character to the right of the insertion point, or delete the selection.

CTRL+DELETE
> Delete text to the end of the line.

F7
> Display the Spelling dialog box.

SHIFT+F2
> Edit a cell comment.

ENTER
> Complete a cell entry and select the next cell below.

CTRL+Z
> Undo the last action.

ESC
> Cancel a cell entry.

CTRL+SHIFT+Z
> When the AutoCorrect Smart Tags is displayed, undo or redo the last automatic correction.

Insert, delete, and copy cells:

CTRL+C
> Copy the selected cells.

CTRL+C, immediately followed by another CTRL+C
> Display the Microsoft Office Clipboard (multiple copy and paste).

CTRL+X
> Cut the selected cells.

CTRL+V
> Paste copied cells.

DELETE
> Clear the contents of the selected cells.

CTRL+HYPHEN
> Delete the selected cells.

CTRL+SHIFT+PLUS SIGN
> Insert blank cells.

Format data:

ALT+' (apostrophe)
> Display the Style dialog box.

CTRL+1
> Display the Format Cells dialog box.

CTRL+SHIFT+~
> Apply the General number format.

CTRL+SHIFT+$
> Apply the Currency format with two decimal places (negative numbers in parentheses).

CTRL+SHIFT+%
> Apply the Percentage format with no decimal places.

CTRL+SHIFT+^
> Apply the Exponential number format with two decimal places.

CTRL+SHIFT+#
> Apply the Date format with the day, month, and year.

CTRL+SHIFT+@
>   Apply the Time format with the hour and minute, and AM or PM.

CTRL+SHIFT+!
>   Apply the Number format with two decimal places, thousands separator, and minus sign (–) for negative values.

CTRL+B
>   Apply or remove bold formatting.

CTRL+I
>   Apply or remove italic formatting.

CTRL+U
>   Apply or remove underlining.

CTRL+5
>   Apply or remove strikethrough.

CTRL+9
>   Hide the selected rows.

CTRL+SHIFT+((opening parenthesis)
>   Unhide any hidden rows within the selection.

CTRL+0 (zero)
>   Hide the selected columns.

CTRL+SHIFT+) (closing parenthesis)
>   Unhide any hidden columns within the selection.

CTRL+SHIFT+&
>   Apply the outline border to the selected cells.

CTRL+SHIFT+_
>   Remove the outline border from the selected cells.

Use the Border tab in the Format Cells dialog box:

Press CTRL+1 to display this dialog box.

ALT+T
>   Apply or remove the top border.

ALT+B
>   Apply or remove the bottom border.

ALT+L
>   Apply or remove the left border.

ALT+R
>   Apply or remove the right border.

ALT+H
>   If cells in multiple rows are selected, apply or remove the horizontal divider.

ALT+V
>   If cells in multiple columns are selected, apply or remove the vertical divider.

ALT+D
>   Apply or remove the downward diagonal border.

ALT+U
>   Apply or remove the upward diagonal border.

Keys for Fltering, Outlining, and Managing Lists

Use data forms (Data menu, Form command):

DOWN ARROW
> Move to the same field in the next record.

UP ARROW
> Move to the same field in the previous record.

TAB and SHIFT+TAB
> Move to each field in the record, then to each command button.

ENTER
> Move to the first field in the next record.

SHIFT+ENTER
> Move to the first field in the previous record.

PAGE DOWN
> Move to the same field 10 records forward.

CTRL+PAGE DOWN
> Start a new, blank record.

PAGE UP
> Move to the same field 10 records back.

CTRL+PAGE UP
> Move to the first record.

HOME or END
> Move to the beginning or end of a field.

SHIFT+END
> Extend selection to the end of a field.

SHIFT+HOME
> Extend selection to the beginning of a field.

LEFT ARROW or RIGHT ARROW
> Move one character left or right within a field.

SHIFT+LEFT ARROW
> Select the character to the left within a field.

SHIFT+RIGHT ARROW
> Select the character to the right within a field.

Filter lists (Data menu, AutoFilter command):

ALT+DOWN ARROW
> In the cell that contains the drop-down Arrow, displays the AutoFilter list for the current column.

DOWN ARROW
> Selects the next item in the AutoFilter list.

UP ARROW
> Selects the previous item in the AutoFilter list.

ALT+UP ARROW
> Closes the AutoFilter list for the current column.

HOME
>   Selects the first item (All) in the AutoFilter list.

END
>   Selects the last item in the AutoFilter list.

ENTER
>   Filters the list based on the item selected from the AutoFilter list.

Show, hide, and outline data:

ALT+SHIFT+RIGHT ARROW
>   Groups rows or columns.

ALT+SHIFT+LEFT ARROW
>   Ungroups rows or columns.

CTRL+8
>   Displays or hides the outline symbols.

CTRL+9
>   Hides the selected rows.

CTRL+SHIFT+((opening parenthesis)
>   Unhides any hidden rows within the selection.

CTRL+0 (zero)
>   Hides the selected columns.

CTRL+SHIFT+) (closing parenthesis)
>   Unhides any hidden columns within the selection.

Keys for PivotTable and PivotChart Reports

Lay out a report onscreen:

1. Press F10 to make the menu bar active.

2. Press CTRL+TAB or CTRL+SHIFT+TAB to make the PivotTable Field List active.

3. Press the DOWN ARROW or UP ARROW key to select the field you want. Press RIGHT ARROW or LEFT ARROW to open or close a field that can be expanded.

4. Press TAB to select the Add To list, and then press DOWN ARROW to open the list.

5. Press DOWN ARROW or UP ARROW to select the area where you want to move the field, and then press ENTER.

6. Press TAB to select the Add To button, and then press ENTER.

Use the PivotTable and PivotChart Wizard–Layout dialog box:

To display this dialog box, press TAB until Layout is selected in Step 3 of the PivotTable and PivotChart Wizard.

UP ARROW or DOWN ARROW
>   Selects the previous or next field button in the list on the right.

LEFT ARROW or RIGHT ARROW
>   With two or more columns of field buttons, selects the button to the left or right.

ALT+R
    Moves the selected field into the Row area.
ALT+C
    Moves the selected field into the Column area.
ALT+D
    Moves the selected field into the Data area.
ALT+P
    Moves the selected field into the Page area.
ALT+L
    Displays the PivotTable Field dialog box for the selected field.

Display and hide items in a field:

ALT+DOWN ARROW
    Displays the drop-down list for a field in a PivotTable or PivotChart report. Use the
    Arrow keys to select the field.
UP ARROW
    Selects the previous item in the list.
DOWN ARROW
    Selects the next item in the list.
RIGHT ARROW
    For an item that has lower-level items available, displays the lower-level items.
LEFT ARROW
    For an item that has lower-level items displayed, hides the lower-level items.
HOME
    Selects the first visible item in the list.
END
    Selects the last visible item in the list.
ENTER
    Closes the list and displays the selected items.
SPACEBAR
    Checks, double-checks, or clears a check box in the list. Double-check selects both an
    item and all of its lower-level items.
TAB
    Switches between the list, the OK button, and the Cancel button.

Change the layout of a report:

CTRL+SHIFT+* (asterisk)
    Selects an entire PivotTable report.
ALT+SHIFT+RIGHT ARROW
    Groups the selected items in a PivotTable field.
ALT+SHIFT+LEFT ARROW
    Ungroups grouped items in a PivotTable field.

Keys for Charts

Create charts and select chart elements:

F11 or ALT+F1
>	Creates a chart of the data in the current range.

CTRL+PAGE DOWN
>	Selects a chart sheet: selects the next sheet in the workbook, until the chart sheet you want is selected.

CTRL+PAGE UP
>	Selects a chart sheet: selects the previous sheet in the workbook, until the chart sheet you want is selected.

DOWN ARROW
>	Selects the previous group of elements in a chart.

UP ARROW
>	Selects the next group of elements in a chart.

RIGHT ARROW
>	Selects the next element within a group.

LEFT ARROW
>	Selects the previous element within a group.

Select an embedded chart:

1.	Display the Drawing toolbar: Press ALT+V, press T, press DOWN ARROW until Drawing is selected, and then press ENTER.

2.	Press F10 to make the menu bar active.

3.	Press CTRL+TAB or CTRL+SHIFT+TAB to select the Drawing toolbar.

4.	Press the RIGHT ARROW key to select the Select Objects button on the Drawing toolbar.

5.	Press CTRL+ENTER to select the first object.

6.	Press the TAB key to cycle forward (or SHIFT+TAB to cycle backward) through the objects until round sizing handles appear on the embedded chart you want to select.

7.	Press CTRL+ENTER to make the chart active so that you can select elements within it.

www.ingramcontent.com/pod-product-compliance
Lightning Source LLC
Chambersburg PA
CBHW080412060326
40689CB00019B/4222